**Bottled
Up**

Dr John McMahon and Lou Lewis

Bottled Up

HOW TO SURVIVE LIVING WITH A PROBLEM DRINKER

LION

Copyright © 2010 Dr John McMahon and Lou Lewis
This edition copyright © 2010 Lion Hudson
The authors assert the moral right
to be identified as the authors of this work

A Lion Book
an imprint of
Lion Hudson plc
Wilkinson House, Jordan Hill Road,
Oxford OX2 8DR, England
www.lionhudson.com
ISBN 978 0 7459 5515 5

Distributed by:
UK: Marston Book Services, PO Box 269, Abingdon, Oxon, OX14 4YN
USA: Trafalgar Square Publishing, 814 N. Franklin Street, Chicago, IL 60610
USA Christian Market: Kregel Publications, PO Box 2607, Grand Rapids, MI
49501

First edition 2010
10 9 8 7 6 5 4 3 2 1 0
All rights reserved

Acknowledgments

Scripture quotations taken from the *Holy Bible, New International Version*,
copyright © 1973, 1978, 1984 International Bible Society. Used by permission of
Zondervan and Hodder & Stoughton Limited. All rights reserved. The 'NIV' and
'New International Version' trademarks are registered in the United States Patent
and Trademark Office by International Bible Society. Use of either trademark
requires the permission of International Bible Society. UK trademark number
1448790.

This book has been printed on paper and board independently certified
as having been produced from sustainable forests.
A catalogue record for this book is available
from the British Library
Typeset in 10/14 Georgia
Printed and bound in Great Britain by CPI Cox & Wyman, Reading.

Contents

Introduction

Many of the audience came up afterwards to thanks us. Some of them said very encouraging and positive things, and there was a lot of emotion flying round the room. It had been quite an amazing day and we were relieved and exhilarated, exhausted but tremendously energized. For both of us, the past few days had been a liberating experience.

Secrecy, shame, guilt, and fear of disapproval were familiar companions for us. Here we were: we had just delivered a public seminar on the *Bottled Up* programme. The people in the audience were mostly professional therapists with their own practices. There were also some individuals who had been attracted by the advance publicity in the newspapers and on the radio. Both of us had stepped out from our professional personas. We had talked about our personal experiences and we had carried out a bit of role play, again from personal experience. The result? A wonderful reception, and feedback and evaluations to die for.

A couple of days earlier, after a lot of internal agonizing, Lou had disclosed that she had lived with a problem drinker for twenty-nine years. That is a difficult task for most people. Lou did it on national radio! Most of her friends and clients did not suspect her burden.

John had spent years lecturing to students and giving papers at national and international conferences. During that time his secret had been well hidden: few people suspected that John had once been a hopeless drunk and drug user, or that since being hospitalized in 1984 he has been clean and sober.

So for both of us this was an especially poignant day. Indeed, for the seminar participants it seems to have been special too. It is a wonderful realization that your experiences and troubles are no longer a burden of shame but can instead be a key to set others free. This shame, which we had spent so long hiding, could now be declared proudly as a means to help other people. Our triumph was not that we were wonderful presenters but rather that we had shared our pain and struggles.

What made that possible was not only, as they say, that we had "walked the walk", but that we had scientific knowledge and the experience of being therapists as well. Having experience alone can, for some people, be very limiting and make them narrow-minded (they sometimes believe that everyone is exactly the same as themselves). Having a broader context – knowledge based on study and professional practice – to inform and embed that experience brings balance. The result can be something very powerful. We hope that you find that power for yourself in this book. However, before you get too far into the programme let us introduce ourselves.

Who are we?

Lou says

I am a singer/songwriter and counsellor living in south-west England. I have two children, now in their early twenties, and was married to my first husband for nearly thirty years. He was a good man, who really loved me and his family, and did everything in his power to enable and support my singing career, which at one stage of my life was pretty successful, doing TV work, recording albums, and performing regular concerts.

Between us, however, we had a dark secret that only those very close to us had any idea about. My husband had a real problem with alcohol. When he drank, which he did on a regular basis, his intake was too high and it affected his behaviour, particularly in the evenings. When he tried to do without it, he managed for a while. He would then go on binges that left the entire household traumatized and distressed.

Don't get me wrong: when I look back, I see how badly I handled the situation at first. Understandably, I was angry, so I screamed and shouted. Understandably, I was upset, so I sobbed and pleaded. Understandably, I felt helpless, so I bullied and threatened. Understandably, I felt betrayed by the lies and broken promises, so I sulked and withdrew from him. Understandably, I was confused because I knew he loved me, so I felt that if I could find the right words, the right plea, the right moment, the right sort of help, *he would change* and our family life would be saved. I dedicated my life, on one level, to making him better, and it felt, at times, that he was dedicating his life to evading my help.

My situation began to improve (sometimes quite considerably) when I started to identify and own self-defeating cycles and put my energies into areas open to change and growth. My husband died sadly (but courageously) of cancer in 2007. By then we had learned to reduce the problems that drinking was causing, and the stormy times, though not completely absent, were much less frequent and nowhere near as devastating for me or my family.

Although my circumstances have changed dramatically over the last few years since his death, these years have shaped the person I am now and they have left me with two strong legacies: a deep empathy with those who walk this particular path and a desire, in some way, to reach out with help, maybe information, but definitely support, understanding, connection, and interaction. I want to help with directing people's energy away from what is elusive to what is possible, helpful, and life-changing.

John says

In 1994 I graduated with a PhD in psychology from the University of Glasgow. My wife and my mother looked on proudly as I paraded in my rented gown (I didn't want to return it afterwards). The sun shone and everyone had strawberries and champagne on the lawn; everyone but me, that is. Few people realized that behind this very happy scene was a story that was best summed up by the wife of my supervisor when she said that I had gone from "a drunk to a doctor in a decade".

I was in a good place: I had a couple of jobs to choose from and had been awarded a large grant to continue my research. I spent the next fifteen years on research, teaching at master's and doctoral level. I wrote papers for prestigious journals and regularly presented work at conferences around the world. I also helped organizations to train therapists and design their treatment regimes.

However, the one thing I kept secret through all of this was my own past and my experience with alcohol and drugs. For about fifteen years I had used alcohol and drugs heavily. In fact, I was treated on numerous occasions by my doctor for alcohol problems, and he consistently suggested that I should attend A A. I disagreed. Finally, I was hospitalized in a dreadful state. The doctor treating me diagnosed brain damage and liver damage and gave me six months to live if I did not stop drinking.

From that day onwards I attended hospital, AA, group therapy, and anything else that was available and I have been clean and sober since – over twenty-five years now. I went back to studying, completed an honours degree in Psychology and then a PhD. My intention was to get away from alcohol and drugs, but even in my studies I was drawn to them. In fact, my thesis was an investigation of what motivated people to stop drinking!

All through my academic years I hid the fact that I had had a drink problem. I did not hide it because of the shame or stigma. No: I hid it because I wanted to be taken seriously as a researcher and an academic, which I was. Ironically, now I find that this personal experience may be one of the most powerful qualifications I have to help people.

Lou and John say

As you can imagine, when we came together as a couple (it is a long story that we may share with you one day), we talked a lot about alcohol and its effect on our lives. Obviously, we were coming at this topic from different perspectives: Lou's was suffering from her husband's drinking and John's suffering was self-inflicted. Then the counsellor and the academic also kicked in and, all in all, the subject was examined from every angle.

We found that we both learned a great deal from each other. Lou learned how her very understandable reactions (described above) would be received by a drinker and why they did not have the effect that she wanted. John learned about how his behaviours had probably impacted his ex-wife and how important the issue of trust was to the relationship.

The more we talked (and we *did* talk a lot), the more we recognized that others might benefit from our experiences. We recognized also that our combination of qualifications and experience might not be unique but they are certainly not common. This fusion of experience and theory, research and training, life-history and therapeutic intervention, and backgrounds and perspectives from both sides, makes a powerful combination.

These talks led us to try to make best use of this fusion by mapping out a programme of change that was solid and workable but also flexible enough to capture the individual differences of people's life circumstances. We call this programme *Bottled Up* and introduce it in this book. It is a programme that is simple in essence but can grow with you. It is designed to help you to take a different approach to your problems and to arrive at new solutions.

What to expect from this book

In this book we want to show you strategies that will help to change the quality of your life. First, we want to give you the tools to re-evaluate your own life. These strategies should help you to feel that you are more in control of your life, that you are more empowered within yourself and in your home. We will urge you to be less isolated and to build yourself a network that can support you and provide a new dimension to your life. Finally, this book will give you tools to help you change your relationship with your drinker and, it is hoped, his drinking, although we cannot guarantee that outcome as it depends on too many factors.

There are six main goals underpinning the *Bottled Up* approach to living with a problem drinker; these are listed below:

1. *We believe that safety/survival is of paramount importance.*
2. *This approach attempts to preserve relationships.*
3. *It aims to help you to alleviate problems by viewing them in a more comprehensive and meaningful way.*
4. *It coaches you on how to change your living conditions.*
5. *It attempts to empower you to live a fulfilling life, independent of his drinking.*
6. *It aims to help you to promote a productive dialogue with the drinker.*

We will discuss these goals in greater detail later in the book.

The nature of change

Why people change is not a secret, nor is it complicated. They change because what they are doing is harming them or because by changing they can have something better. You may be disagreeing (quite strongly even) with that last sentence. You may be saying that he[1] has been harming himself for years and has made no move to change. In fact, you have pointed out on numerous occasions how much he is harming himself and he still hasn't changed!

There could be a number of reasons for that, and we will explore some of them in this book. However, we have to accept that everyone is different. Some things that are acceptable risks for one person are quite unacceptable for another. An easily understandable example of that is the kind of sports that people choose. Some people love boxing, wrestling, and martial arts, whereas that kind of risk or pain would be unthinkable for others. It is not very different with the consequences of alcohol. Some people feel that there is either no risk or little risk associated with their drinking, even though their close friends or relatives feel that they are clearly harming themselves.

---

1 Please note that we will use "he" when talking about the drinker because the majority of problem drinkers are male (although the gap is closing). This is not through any sort of chauvinism or because we do not recognize that women can also be problem drinkers: we do. We are using this convention as it is easier to use just one gender and we do not want to alternate "he" and "she" as this becomes cumbersome to read after a while.

Another reason why people do not change is that they may be being protected from the negative consequences of their drinking. Perhaps you look after your drinker to make sure that he is safe. Maybe you clean up after him and protect him by keeping his drinking secret. If he is not experiencing the negative consequences of drinking, he will be less likely to change.

In this book we will show you strategies that you can adopt to make it more likely that your drinker will change. To help this process along, it is likely that you will need to change your own behaviour. This may be confusing at first. Why should *you* change? You are not the one with the problem.

It is easy to believe the drinker is the one with the problem and that you are just the helpless onlooker or even the victim. As we discuss at some length in the next chapter, the problem is one that is shared by both of you. He may be the problem drinker, but you are having problems with his drinking. You may have noticed that there are things you do that have an impact on his drinking. He may cut back or even stop for a time after you have a row or after a particularly bad binge. Or it may be that the only effect you seem to have on his drinking is to make it worse.

We want you to start to think of his drinking not as something entirely independent of you but as something that you can affect. Try to think of his drinking and your reactions as a dance. At the moment he is leading the dance and you are following along. We want to show you how first to stop following his lead and then to lead the dance yourself so that your steps come to affect his steps.

CHAPTER 1

Whose problem is it anyway?

We're not sure where you are reading this book but we are fairly sure that your drinker is not nearby and probably does not know that you have it. When you saw it in the shop, you probably flicked through it, then made straight for this chapter. You may still be in the shop and you haven't bought the book yet. You desperately want to know the answer to the question that is constantly in your head.

Last night you were feeling guilty. You had been surfing the internet again. You had been furtively looking at those websites again while he was out. You always cover your tracks in case he finds out, otherwise there will be a terrible row – again. You need to look, you need the information, but still you feel that you are betraying him. Maybe this time you will get what you want: satisfaction, answers.

You typed "Is my husband an alcoholic?" and hit search. You remembered the last conversation you had about that issue (for "conversation", read "screaming fight"). It started because he had got drunk again, and you had suggested that he might have a problem with his drinking. He immediately became hurt, insulted, and defensive, and denied any problem. The "conversation" then deteriorated.

To be more precise, it became rather jumbled and words such as "neurotic" and "alcoholic" were thrown about. He stormed off to nurse his wounded pride, somewhere where there was a supply of alcohol, and you were left frazzled, frustrated, and impotent.

You knew that you were right. He does have a problem! He has shown that over and over. He cannot be trusted to turn up on time and sober. He can't control his drinking. If there is alcohol around, he will drink it and won't stop till it's finished or he is drunk. OK, as he pointed out, it doesn't happen every time; there are times when he doesn't get drunk. In fact, there are times when he doesn't even drink at all. But – and it's a big but – when he does drink...

So here you are trying to find evidence to support what you already believe: that he needs to reduce his drinking or, better still, stop altogether. The website information was useful but inconclusive. There appear to be so many different varieties of drinking problems. There is the alcoholic, the dependent drinker, the hazardous drinker, the alcohol abuser, the alcohol misuser, and the binger. So it is difficult to pin down a definition that you can use in your next "discussion". It needs to be clear and irrefutable. Maybe then he will listen to you and realize what he is doing to you, his family, and himself. You know that if you can only make him see the problem, he will change.

If you identify with some or all of the above, you can relax. You have found what you are looking for: a clear and irrefutable definition of drinking problems. We will show you how to carry out the assessment and how to use and present the results to change your life and the behaviour of your drinker. However, first let's look at what happens in alcohol treatment units.

Why do you want a definition?

If you have a clear and irrefutable definition, how is it going to help you and your partner? You probably believe that showing your drinker the definition or evidence you have found will convince him of his problem. He will then see his error and will change his ways. Sounds logical, doesn't it?

One small problem: how many times have you tried this strategy in the past? How many times have you pointed out that he was drunk, rude, irresponsible, wasteful? How many times has it been successful? If you are reading this book, then we know the answer! So why would it be successful this time?

Unfortunately, the belief that having a definitive diagnosis will result in him changing is almost certainly flawed. Not that long ago, almost all alcohol treatment units would insist that people identify themselves as being alcoholics before treatment would even begin. Many clients were so resistant to calling themselves alcoholics that some units even had special procedures aimed at breaking down their resistance or denial. These procedures consisted of shouting at and trying to force the drinker to admit his problem. Does this sound familiar? It should. It was based on exactly the same belief that most partners have: if only the drinker can admit that he is an alcoholic (has a problem), then he will change.

Many (but not all) alcohol treatment units have moved away from this kind of approach. They have done so because they found that such methods often made their clients even more resistant to change. So the modern approach to treating alcohol problems does not rely on any admission of being an alcoholic; instead, it relies more on changing the drinker's motivations, so that drinking looks less attractive. The method we will show you in this book is based on this new approach.

Yes, but does he have a problem?

To answer that question, let us tell you a story – a true story. It is called "Dangerous Danny and the Wrong Rain". Just over a year ago we decided to invest in a lodge in a country park in Devon.

So we picked out a lovely lodge, in a quiet spot with a great view. We loved it. Then we had some real UK summer weather – torrential rain! For two days it rained and rained, and rained some more. In the midst of this we noticed that we had water running down from the central heating boiler – not good, we thought. The lodge was under guarantee for a year, however, so it was someone else's responsibility to fix the problem.

A quick phone call brought the maintenance manager (good), whom other workmen discreetly called Dangerous Danny (less good). He looked in the cupboard, then did what all tradesmen seem to do: he tutted a lot, huffed a lot, scratched his head a lot, and looked worried a lot.

Eventually, he acknowledged that we were there and told us we had a leak. Well, he just soared in my estimation; the man was obviously a genius. His next words confirmed that status. "The problem is that it's the wrong rain!"

Danny then launched into an explanation that was either the ravings of a madman or (as we said before) pure genius. We both consider ourselves well-educated, but halfway through the explanation we thought that he had lapsed into ancient Armenian or some obscure dialect of Klingon. We looked at each other to see if the other understood it any better. Nope!

"Er, can you fix it?" we asked. "Oh yes, all it needs is a bit of filler." We both grinned. We understood that bit and it was good news. Two days later he returned with some filler and we have never had a drip since.

You are probably thinking "Yes, all very nice, but what has that got to do with me and my problem drinker?" Well, it is a very similar situation to the one you and your drinker are in.

You have been under the impression that you needed to have a diagnosis and an understanding of the drinker's status (alcoholic, dependent) to get things to change. What you found was even more confusing (DD's explanation of the wrong rain). Perhaps the most important question is not "Is he an alcoholic, problem drinker, or whatever?" but rather "How can we get him to change?" Again, it was only when we asked DD if our leak could be fixed that he made any sense.

Blaming, naming, shaming, and framing

All right, then, can it be fixed? The short answer to that question is yes, it can. However, it does require patience, persistence, and putting in the effort. One of the first things that needs to happen is a change in you. There needs to be a change of thinking and, as we shall see later in the book, a change in your actions and reactions to the drinker.

Wait! Hold it! Before you throw this book across the room swearing about "just what I need: more guilt", please read on. We are not shifting the blame to you; we just want to show you new behaviours that will make change in your drinker much more likely than it is at the moment. Remember the dance analogy in the Introduction.

The first change that needs to take place is your view of the problem. If you are reading this book, it's likely that you believe that he has a problem. You don't need anyone to tell you that your partner got drunk and embarrassed everyone, especially you; that he stops for a drink on the way home from work instead of arriving at the time agreed; that your dad would rather go drinking than spend time with his family; that he is embarrassingly drunk when your boyfriend or other friends visit. You know these things because they happen to you. You don't need anyone to tell you that there is a problem any more than we needed DD to tell us we had a leak.

You know there is a problem and you know that drinking is involved. You would like to put a name to it – such as alcoholism. If you could do that, then he would be shamed into changing. Seems logical. In this book, however, what we ask you to do instead is look at it in a different way – what psychologists call reframing.

The problem is not his alone. It is a problem that affects you as well. You don't need a diagnosis to tell you that you are angry, frustrated, depressed, anxious, or miserable. His drinking is affecting your relationship and could be having an adverse affect on your health, mental and physical.

You do not need a diagnosis to determine whether he is an alcoholic, a dependent drinker, or a binger. You know the effect his drinking is having on your relationship, your family, your health. That is a sufficient diagnosis and we will show you how to make a thorough assessment and use it to promote changes in your life.

Definition

Maybe it would be useful to examine definitions of drinking problems in the light of modern thinking. First of all, the term "alcoholism" is one that is decreasingly used in professional circles these days. One of the main reasons is the huge controversy that tends to surround the actual term. More commonly used terms are alcohol abuse and alcohol dependence. Definitions of both conditions, as laid out in *DSM IV* (*Diagnostic Statistical Manual* – the official manual for diagnosis, currently in use by psychologists) can be found below.

DSM-IV Diagnostic Criteria for Alcohol Abuse

1. A maladaptive pattern of alcohol abuse leading to clinically significant impairment or distress, as manifested by one or more of the following, occurring within a twelve-month period:

   a) Recurrent alcohol use resulting in failure to fulfil major role obligations at work, school, or home (for example, repeated absences or poor work performance related to substance use; substance-related absences, suspensions, or expulsions from school; or neglect of children or household).

   b) Recurrent alcohol use in situations in which it is physically hazardous (for example, driving an automobile or operating a machine).

   c) Recurrent alcohol-related legal problems (for example, arrests for alcohol-related disorderly conduct).

   d) Continued alcohol use despite persistent or

> *recurrent social or interpersonal problems*
> *caused or exacerbated by the effects of the alcohol*
> *(for example, arguments with spouse about*
> *consequences of intoxication or physical fights).*

2. These symptoms must never have met the criteria for
   alcohol dependence.

Thus the main features of alcohol abuse are using alcohol
often and in a reckless or dangerous manner.

DSM-IV Diagnostic Criteria for Alcohol Dependence

A maladaptive pattern of alcohol use, leading to clinically
significant impairment or distress, as manifested by three
or more of the following seven criteria, occurring at any
time in the same twelve-month period:

1. Tolerance, as defined by either of the following:
   a) A need for markedly increased amounts of alcohol
      to achieve intoxication or desired effect.
   b) Markedly diminished effect with continued use of
      the same amount of alcohol.

2. Withdrawal, as defined by either of the following:
   a) The characteristic withdrawal syndrome for
      alcohol (refer to DSM-IV for further details).
   b) Alcohol is taken to relieve or avoid withdrawal
      symptoms.

3. Alcohol is often taken in larger amounts or over a
   longer period than was intended.

4. There is a persistent desire or there are unsuccessful
   efforts to cut down or control alcohol use.

5. A great deal of time is spent in activities necessary to obtain alcohol, use alcohol, or recover from its effects.

6. Important social, occupational, or recreational activities are given up or reduced because of alcohol use.

7. Alcohol use is continued despite knowledge of having a persistent or recurrent physical or psychological problem that is likely to have been caused or exacerbated by the alcohol (for example, continued drinking despite recognition that an ulcer was made worse by alcohol consumption).

As you can see, the criteria for dependence are much more about the "need" to drink and the physiological changes that appear to be occurring. This term "dependence" tends to replace the previous term "alcoholism".

CHAPTER 2

Why?

Your partner comes home unsteady on his feet. The smell of alcohol is overpowering. Every time he opens his mouth, another wave of boozy smell washes over you and his eyes are glazed. But when you say "You have been drinking!" quick as a flash back comes the reply "No I haven't."

It's frustrating, it's infuriating, it's insulting, it's stupid. No wonder there is a saying in AA: "How do you know an alcoholic is lying? His lips are moving." So why does he lie so often, so badly, at all?

You have probably come to this book looking for answers about why he behaves the way he does. Why does he lie? Why does he deny he has a problem when everyone else can see it so clearly? Denial and lying are two of the topics that we address in this chapter as we try to provide some insight into the nature of problem drinking and addiction. We look at some of the recent research and what it has to tell us about drinking and change. As far as possible, we have tried to present this discussion in a non-technical way. So please don't just skip over this chapter! If you are going to understand the rationale of the *Bottled Up* approach that we present in later chapters, it would be useful to spend some time reading this chapter and the explanations that it offers.

Is problem drinking a disease?

This question is one of the most hotly contested issues in the alcohol and drug field. In the last thirty years the majority of the evidence that has been collected suggests that it is not a disease, or at least not in the way that we would normally think of a disease. Nevertheless, there are large numbers of people who firmly believe it is a disease and are not swayed in any way by the evidence. At present there seems to be no way of reconciling the two viewpoints.

In respect of someone changing their drinking behaviour, it is immaterial whether or not it is a disease: they still have to reduce their intake or stop altogether. However, many of the accompanying behaviours of problem drinking are blamed on a disease and that is not always very helpful. We will try to explain some of these behaviours in terms of the function they serve, rather than attributing them to some pathological condition. That way we can perhaps understand these behaviours for what they are and address them.

"The lies are almost worse than the drinking!"

This is something we often hear from partners of problem drinkers. They have said that at least they felt they knew where they were with the drinking, but the lying sometimes made them doubt themselves and their sanity.

One of the unfortunate consequences of continual lies may be that you stop believing anything he says. Your trust may become eroded and with it your respect for him, and that may be replaced with contempt. Let's look a bit more at the kind of lies he tells and why he lies.

For most drinkers, if you look at the type of lies they tell, you find that they are all (or nearly all) associated with alcohol. They are generally in response to a question or an accusation about their drinking – for example, whether they have been drinking and how much. The frequency of lies told when not being questioned about consumption is almost certainly much less. What it appears to show is that a drinker's lying is quite selective, that is it is used to protect drinking and escape the possibility of having to admit that alcohol is a problem.

However, the notion that lying is part of a disease of alcoholism, that the lies could be so specific, is a bit implausible. It would be a rather strange disease that would make a person lie only when he talks about one subject and be truthful when talking about anything else. Instead, the lying would seem to be what psychologists call "functional". What that means is that it is used for a specific purpose, which is, consciously or unconsciously, to protect the drinking.

Remember that the drinker gets some benefit from drinking. Mostly the benefits are to do with how it makes the drinker feel. Research on what drinkers (*all* drinkers, not just problem drinkers) expect when they drink alcohol has found that they believe they will:

- be more sociable

- find it easier to talk to people

- be sexier, more powerful, more relaxed

- be able to say what they want, more confident

- generally feel better and find the world a better and less boring place.

That is only part of the list but, if that is what they expect, it is easy to see why people would want to drink.

We need to remember that alcohol is a powerful drug. It can change how we feel about ourselves and the world. The same research found that the more positive things that people expect to get from alcohol, the more they tended to drink. More importantly, research found that the more people valued these positive things, the more likely they were to drink heavily. In other words, if he believes that drinking alcohol can help him talk to people and be more popular at a party, and this is important to him, then it is easy to see why he might drink to excess. For if a little drink will make him a bit popular, then a big drink will make him really popular. Or if a young man believes that alcohol makes him sexier and more attractive to females, then he might drink more to help him attract women. An important fact found by the research was that the expectation does not need to be true. What is important is that if he believes that he will gain these effects, he will be encouraged to drink. Indeed, most of the beliefs we hold about alcohol are untrue: alcohol is not actually capable of producing these effects. Does he really think that alcohol makes him sexier or a better singer?

The danger is that because of these lies you may treat the drinker as a pathological liar in all spheres of life and distrust anything he says. In actual fact, he may be extremely honest and, ironically, may even pride himself on that honesty. However, when it comes to alcohol, the truth may be in short supply. Why should that be?

As we suggested above, the lies are less about misleading and more about avoiding having to answer or face tough questions. Alcohol is a valuable ally and it needs to be defended. The lies tend to be the types that are aimed at closing down a conversation rather than opening one up. The subtext of the lie is "Go away and stop asking me difficult questions; I don't want to answer these questions." He may not even realize that he is doing it sometimes, although at other times he clearly does.

When he lies to you, you may feel that you need to get him to admit that he has been lying. But to pursue this goal may cost you more emotionally than you gain. For if the drinker is lying and has been drinking, to pursue the "truth" is a pointless exercise. He will become more entrenched in the lie and continue to defend it, and you will become more frustrated and infuriated. You probably know all that you need to know already. Remember, you have the evidence of your own senses: you can see and smell if he has been drinking. Try not to make an issue of it as it will just arouse negative feelings in you and increase your sense of frustration and powerlessness. Let it go – it is a pointless pursuit!

No, we are not encouraging or condoning his lies. Nor are we trying to ignore the distress that they cause you. We are just being pragmatic. Concentrate your energy on doing things that will bring results rather than hitting your head against a brick wall. In the next chapter we will discuss some of the brick walls that you may have been trying to break down with your head. The later chapters will then introduce new ways of behaving that will make change much more likely.

In those later chapters we encourage you to remember

the good things about your drinker, what initially attracted you to him, what you love about him. You can decide to spend time with the non-drinking person you love and withdraw from the drinking person who frustrates and infuriates you. We discuss these issues when we introduce the *Bottled Up* tools – LOVE, SHARE, and HOPE.

Denial

As we discussed previously, some argue that alcoholism, like any other addiction, is a disease. They suggest that there are certain characteristics that are integral to that disease, such as craving, loss of control, and, of course, denial. Denial is a person's apparent inability to recognize or admit that he has a problem with alcohol. It is believed to be a defence mechanism that allows the alcoholic to continue with his behaviour, despite the negative consequences and the fact that it is obvious to everyone else that he has a problem.

In the past you or someone else may have challenged him about his drinking, about whether he had a problem. You may have used the term "alcoholic" or you may have suggested, perhaps very strongly, that he should see someone about his drinking. At that point you may have (almost certainly) met the "denial process" – "I'm not an alcoholic, I don't need to see anyone!" Why does he not see what you see: the problems that his drinking causes, the changes in his personality and behaviour?

There are two main reasons why this happens. The first of these is due to what psychologists call "reactance". Basically, what this means is that people (not just addicts) have a natural tendency to defend themselves if they are accused and feel threatened in any way. If someone made a remark about your appearance – for example, suggesting you are getting fat – you would probably feel yourself bristle with indignation and would deny it, even if you had gained a few pounds. Or if someone accused you of being rude, again you may feel insulted and misunderstood. This is what reactance means. It is the apparent natural tendency that we have to defend ourselves from perceived threat, and it happens even if there is some truth or justification in the perceived threat.

The same processes are at work in what some people would call "alcoholic denial". When heavy drinkers are accused of being alcoholics, there is a natural reactance that occurs. It is not necessarily that they do not or cannot recognize a problem; it is that the approach is too direct. Later in the book we will show you a different approach that avoids the direct accusation and, we hope, the denial too.

The second reason for denial may be that he genuinely does not recognize that he has a problem. You might find that hard to believe, but it may well be true. In the early 1980s two American psychologists, James Prochaska and Carlo DiClemente, published a paper describing the stages that people went through on their journey of change. The first of these stages they called "precontemplation" (not thinking about change). They describe the person in this stage as someone who does not recognize a problem, even though others believe that there is one. In their research they found that the critical condition for the person moving from being a precontemplator to being a contemplator (thinking about change) was when the negatives (the cons) of drinking began to outweigh the positives (the pros) of drinking.

This paper and other research of that time began to change the way addiction was treated. Previously, people who came to treatment apparently in denial and so unmotivated to change, were dismissed and told to return when they were motivated. They were regarded as precontemplators. This meant that it is the treatment centre's job to try to motivate the drinker by getting him to re-examine the pros and cons of his drinking. The aim is that the drinker will start to recognize a problem as he sees a change in the balance of the pros and cons of drinking.

Your drinker is no different. If he is going to be motivated to change, then it is important that he begins to recognize the negatives of his drinking. You may say that you have pointed them out to him countless times, but he does not pay a blind bit of notice. The problem is that pointing them out leads to the reactance that we considered above. What is important is that he comes to recognize the negatives himself. Counsellors have developed sophisticated techniques to achieve this shift in motivation which have been shown to have some success. We are not asking or suggesting that you learn these techniques. You can achieve a shift in motivation using a different technique.

People can change their level of motivation in two ways. First, they can re-examine the consequences (both positive and negative) of drinking. Second, they can start to experience more negatives, which will also cause the balance to shift. It is the second of these methods that you will be using. At present you may be protecting the drinker from some of the negative consequences of his drinking, and the result of that protection may be that he does not recognize the extent of the problem. We will examine this more fully in later chapters and show you how you can detach from his drinking and allow the negative consequences to occur and so help to shift the balance of motivation.

Shame and guilt

People living with a problem drinker are often burdened by feelings of shame and guilt. Shame is a feeling that arises from some dishonourable act or behaviour done by ourselves or others, whereas guilt is a feeling of responsibility for having done something wrong. Both of these feelings are common in your situation.

You may feel shame because you know that this is not how you should be living or want to live. You do not want people to witness your dirty secret, to see him drunk, and to see the feelings that are coursing through you. You feel guilty because deep inside you believe that you should be changing this situation. You may know that it is your duty to make it right, to bring out the potential of your drinker instead of this side of his character that puts alcohol above his devotion to you, his family, and anything else.

People may have already told you that none of this is your fault. You do not make him drink – quite the reverse. You are the one doing your best to try to stop him. You are the one who holds everything together, looks after the family, makes sure the children are safe and well, that the bills are paid, and that there is food on the table. It is great to hear them say this and for a short time it makes you feel better. But the feelings come back and again you feel guilty and ashamed.

Many people handle these feelings by hiding away. They pull up the drawbridge and keep the outside world at bay.

They become secretive and never talk about their lives, their fears, and their problems. They may tell themselves that they are being loyal to the drinker by not discussing his issues. They may realize that they are hiding behind a veil of secrecy, designed purely to ensure that no one suspects that their lives are not normal.

Unfortunately, the best way to handle and combat these feelings is also the one that people in this situation are least likely to do. The more you try to hide your situation, the more it threatens to overwhelm you and the more guilt and shame you feel. Therefore, the best way to handle these feelings is to share the secret with someone else, and more people if possible. But, of course, this is exactly what you have been trying to avoid.

Guilt and shame have power when they are hidden. They feed on our insecurity of being discovered and then rejected when we are found out. In the majority of cases this fear is groundless, and intellectually we may even know that. However, these negative feelings are not grounded in logic. They are the primal fears that lurk in all of us: the fears that we are different, a failure, not good enough, will be rejected, are at fault. Often there is no real form to these fears. If someone asked you "What exactly is it that you are afraid of?" there is a strong possibility that you could not tell them. That is the nature of the fears. They are similar to our fear of the dark and the shadows. We need to bring some light to them. We do that by bringing them out in the open, by telling others about them. That way we face our fears. We test the reality of the lies that the voice in our heads is telling us "No one will like you!" It sets us free and starts to reduce the guilt and shame by putting things back into perspective.

Isolation

Associated with the issue of shame and guilt is isolation. Trying to contain the guilt and shame of the secret that you have a problem drinker in the house becomes increasingly difficult to achieve, particularly with close friends and relatives. You may have found yourself lying to them about what is happening in your life, reluctant to tell them the truth. That brings a guilt all of its own, however, and you have more than enough of that. So the solution is to pull away from your friends. This may happen slowly at first – perhaps by making an excuse when invited to a night out or a party because you feel unable to trust your drinker not to get drunk. These excuses may become the norm until eventually people stop inviting you. There is a relief when that happens, but it comes at a price. That price may be a deep sadness at your loss and may also include a raging resentment at your growing isolation.

The isolation and secrecy soon become a way of life. We called this book and our whole approach *Bottled Up* in recognition of this process. This refers to the range of guilt, shame, and anger that people try to contain through secrecy. When we started the *Bottled Up* website, we hoped to provide a virtual place of safety where people could come and share with each other. So ingrained was the need for secrecy, however, that some people would not use the social networking tools such as the blog or forum. In fact, many of them even turned off their profiles so that they were invisible to the other members. It is a form of behaviour that we understand but which we were longing to break down so that people could connect to others and be free.

In later chapters we will encourage you to socialize, to make a life for yourself and become more independent. This is not selfish or disloyal behaviour. By making a life for yourself outside the home, all of the family will benefit, not just you. It will relieve some of your guilt and shame, reduce your tension, and increase your self-esteem. All of this should lighten your mood and make you less volatile with your drinker and your family. We will discuss this at greater length in Chapter 12.

It's not personal!

It is all too easy to personalize the drinker's behaviour. Many ask the question "How can he drink like that if he loves me?" When viewed in those terms, unfortunately, it is a recipe for a crushing blow to self-esteem. The drinker does not see it in those terms and would be shocked by the question. For him there is no either/or situation involved: he loves you, his family, his home, so what is the problem? For you, however, it probably feels very personal.

Why he drinks will vary from person to person and according to whether or not he is dependent on alcohol. If he is not dependent on alcohol, it may be social pressure, stress, or habit. For dependent drinkers, there is more internal pressure due to the addictive properties of alcohol, and he may be drinking to get rid of or control the withdrawal symptoms. One thing that is unlikely to be going through his mind is weighing up his love for you versus the alcohol.

We will show you in later chapters how to make it personal in the right way. You can use this strategy to encourage change. Part of encouraging change is to provide alternatives to alcohol and to try to rekindle your relationship.

Fear of losing him

The final issue to discuss in this chapter is fear: specifically, fear of him walking out and leaving you. Partners of drinkers often fear that if they say too much or push the drinking issue too far, the drinker will leave. That is a possibility; we can't deny it.

However, if you are in that position, you need to weigh that possibility against the extreme probability of continuing the way you are living now without change. Can you really carry on the way things are, or can you risk his disapproval and leaving? If we look at the statistics on divorce, they show that in over 66 per cent of divorces it was the woman who petitioned for divorce. And one of the most common reasons for divorce is alcohol abuse. So perhaps your fears are less grounded than you believe.

In later chapters we will start to look at ways to reverse the problems we have discussed here. We will show you ways in which you can start to tackle these issues and improve your lifestyle and your physical and mental health. Before we do that, however, we will look at behaviours that may exacerbate some of your problems and hinder change.

CHAPTER 3

The 4 Ps

When people around us behave in a way that we consider to be unreasonable, unacceptable, dangerous, undesirable, or unwanted, we normally try to get them to stop doing whatever it is that they are doing. Most of us have a number of stock responses. These responses are normal, natural, and in some situations they may be the perfect solution.

Generally, we want the person to see our point of view, feel our pain, discomfort, or inconvenience. If we are successful, they will stop doing whatever it is they are doing, or at least not do it to us or around us.

So when the drinker in our lives behaves in an unacceptable way, we feel that the tactics that we have used previously should again be successful. In most cases, however, not only are they not successful, but in fact they often make things much worse. The anger and frustration you feel about his behaviour, what he did or failed to do, is doubled by the fact that all of your usual strategies have little effect (or, worse, the wrong effect) in this situation.

The rules seem to have changed and no one told you. You are powerless. It is frightening. Everything that you have learned and used effectively fails to work in this situation. You have no means of controlling it. Bad things are happening to you. You know deep down inside that this is none of your doing, and yet somehow you feel guilty, responsible.

To deal with the situation, you use the only tools that you have at your disposal. You may see some chinks of light and odd periods of (short-lived) change that give you hope and make you think that your methods do work after all. Ultimately, however, they don't work, or at least they don't work for very long. If this is where you are, be kind to yourself. You are not bad or stupid; you are a human being in a difficult (some might say impossible) situation.

In the rest of the book we will show you alternative ways of handling your situation that are more productive than your present approaches. However, to understand the need for these other approaches and why they work better, we should first look at what doesn't work and why.

We will begin by describing each of the approaches and discuss why they do not have the impact that you intended. To illustrate why these strategies do not work, we have included the "View of the drinker", which gives some indication (based on John's personal experience) of how it feels to be on the receiving end of the 4 Ps: punishing, picking a fight, policing, and pleading.

Punishing

Punishing is a very normal reaction to unreasonable behaviour. If we feel that we have been hurt, then it is natural to want to hurt the person in return so that they feel and understand a part of our hurt. We are not saying that this is the right thing to do or suggesting that it is morally defensible, just that it is an instinct.

Punishment has been used as a way of controlling and changing behaviour since the dawn of time. Different societies inflict pain on, incarcerate, and even kill people who break the rules and behave in a manner that is disapproved of. Some people react positively to the punishment and change; some do not transgress for fear of the punishment. But for others it has little effect. Psychologists have suggested that punishment tends to make people more adept at avoiding punishment, rather than changing their behaviour. An example of this is the speed camera. How many of us exceed the speed limit, slow down for the camera, and speed up again when we have passed it?

In relationships, the form the punishment takes can vary, but it often involves withholding. For example, it can involve withdrawing all communication – the silent treatment – or withholding sex or any form of affection. It can involve stopping any kind of care and attention – for example, no cooking or cleaning. How long this punishment lasts will again vary from person to person. What you need to ask yourself is this: "Does it work? Does it have the desired effect?" May we suggest that the answer to this is no! If it worked, this book would not exist as the alcohol problem would have been eradicated long ago.

View of the drinker

The silent treatment – I hate it but I suppose you just have to accept it as one of the consequences of drinking: hangover and (thankfully) silence. As they say, if you can't do the time, then don't do the crime.

I thought that she had a bit of a point at the beginning: "OK, I admit it, I got drunk, made a fool of myself and you; therefore, I deserve the disapproval."

But now she just goes on a bit. I expect it now. No sex, no cuddles, no meals. It used to make me feel a bit guilty, but now I just feel that it is another example of her unreasonable behaviour. I want to go out with my mates or have a drink in peace. Doesn't mean I don't love her, but, oh no, off she goes like a martyr, dripping self-pity all over the place. I really hate that silent treatment. It makes me feel rejected (well, I am being rejected) and unloved. I mean, no wonder I drink. Do you see what I have to suffer? Anyone would drink in these circumstances.

Picking a fight

Another way of dealing with the situation is to get angry and vent your feelings. Again quite natural, but to expect the drinker to sit passively and listen while you express all the anger and frustration that has been brewing for some time (even years) is probably unrealistic. The result is that you vent and the drinker defends, and you vent some more and the drinker defends some more. Soon the original thread of the discussion is lost in a shouting contest and a full-blown argument is in progress.

The drinker picks up not on your justifiable points but on any inaccuracies, no matter how small. It has to be said that there is nothing and no one more self-righteous than a drinker who has been wrongly accused. You feel confused and frustrated. You feel you were totally justified – he was in the wrong – but somehow, and you're not sure how, he has become the injured party and you find that it is you who is in the wrong.

Not only did he not apologize, beg your forgiveness, and promise to change his ways, but he stormed out to go drinking again. How did that happen?

View of the drinker

Sometimes my wife will pick a fight. She will draw herself up to her full height and then she will add a few inches by standing on her moral high ground. She will fix me with that look specially designed for naughty children, bad smells, and drunken husbands. Then she will start reciting her list of my faults and wrongdoings. Usually, it will start with her in control (barely) but her voice will get louder and more strident as our "conversation" progresses.

When she starts out, I will sometimes (but not often) feel she has a point, and if she would stop there, I would probably say OK, fair point. But it never does stop there as she wants to bring up obscure incidents from years ago. So now I need to defend myself. The Geneva Convention is ripped up and she does not seem to agree that everyone is innocent till proven guilty. Her voice will go up a couple of octaves; I will join in. Now neither of us is listening. We are both talking, very loudly.

It is time to play my trump card. I shout (must get the tone right) that I am misunderstood (or some other phrase that suggests that I am the wronged party). I now have two exit strategies, both rather effective, even if I say so myself. The first is to suggest that I have been wrongly accused of drinking too much, being an alcoholic, or something else about my drinking. Then, in a very wounded manner, I sweep out, saying "Well, I might as well do what I have been accused of". I like that exit. Very melodramatic. It completely wrong-foots her and she keeps falling for it. If I can keep her guilt levels up, then she might back off.

The other exit is to sweep out looking very pained and sad, and saying either "I can't reason with you while you are like that" or "You just don't understand me". This one completely removes the initiative from her and gives me ammunition about how neurotic she is ready for the next fight.

There will be another fight – you can count on it. In fact, sometimes the easiest way for me to get out for a drink is to pick a fight and storm out. I don't think she has realized that yet. At least I hope she hasn't.

Policing

Policing means checking on how much he drinks or spends on drinking and trying to control it. It might involve going to the bar with him or trying to control what he drinks in the house. It could involve marking the level of bottles and checking to see how much has been consumed. This is when the fun really starts.

He will almost certainly want to drink much more than you want him to. So it is his goal to drink and your goal to minimize his drinking. In the bar he may go to the toilet more often than normal. This allows him to get a drink out of your line of sight. He may order extra drinks at the bar so that he drinks one at the bar and brings one to the table.

At home he may start to hide alcohol around the house which he will drink when you are not looking. If you have marked bottles, he will start topping them up with booze from his stash, water, or even cold tea in the whisky bottle.

This "game" of hide-the-booze does little to help the relationship. Trust and truth are obvious victims, but often you may feel that your sanity is suffering as you know he has had much more to drink than he will admit. If only. If only you could find the bottle, then you would be vindicated and he would confess and make changes in his life and drinking. If only. Both of you know that is not going to happen. In fact, it will probably send him to the pub or a store for another drink.

View of the drinker

I wanted her to be my drinking companion. If only she would come to the pub, we could have fun together. Unfortunately, she did come to the pub and it was miserable. "Have you finished that drink already?" "You're not going to have another, are you?" "We've been here for an hour now. Can't we go home yet?"

It was awful. She was watching everything I did, every drink I bought or someone else bought for me. She hardly finished her one drink and just kept wanting to go home. I thought that we might have had a bit of fun, but no. I got some booze to take home and the first thing she said was "Have you not had enough? You are not going to drink all that tonight, are you?"

I'm not going to take her again. I have told her loads of times that I only have a couple of pints. She seemed to take that literally – a couple of pints means two pints! Now she realizes that I drink much more than that. Not good!

Pleading

He says he loves you, but he is not acting as if he loves you. So maybe you could appeal to that love: "If you really loved me and really loved the children, you would not drink like that." If you lay it on thick enough, perhaps he could see what he is doing to you, the children, the home, himself. You know that he is a good man really, and if you could just find the right words, emotions, tears, it would all change.

Unfortunately, it is not that he does not love you or that he does not realize what he is doing. If he truly is addicted to alcohol, then there are powerful forces at work inside him. He is probably full of guilt already. He is probably ashamed by his behaviour. *He does not want to hurt you; he just does not want to hurt.* The alcohol numbs the pain, takes away the guilt, removes the shame.

If you plead with him, it reminds him of the guilt, the shame, his inadequacy. It reminds him of the gulf between what he wants to be and what he is, and that makes drinking a more attractive proposition. Will it stop him drinking? Probably not; in fact, it will probably send him to the pub or a store for another drink.

View of the drinker

I hate it when she pleads. I can stand the arguments, the nagging, and the fights. They are not particularly pleasant but it's what you expect. The pleading, though

– that's different. It gets to me! It makes me feel really
guilty. I don't want to hurt her. I mean, I married her
because I loved her. Remember the vows: to cherish, to
protect. Maybe that wasn't what was said but it's what
I believe. I am the man of the house. I am the protector.
I'm supposed to keep danger and hurt from my home!
But it is me that is causing the hurt.

I feel really bad, really inadequate. Not much of a
man, am I? I really hate myself, hate the drink. But the
only thing that makes me feel better at these times is
having a drink. I wish I wasn't hurting her, but I really
don't want to hurt!

None of this is meant in any way to place the blame for
the drinking on your shoulders. The above responses to
drinking are completely natural reactions and can work
in certain situations. However, the success rate of these
reactions in problem drinking is pretty low. You believe
that you can reach him through these approaches and that
he will see your point and change.

In this chapter we use "View of the drinker" to try to
give you an insight into the mind of the drinker and how
he is reacting to your various approaches. Unfortunately,
as you can see, it may not be the way you anticipated.

That is why we suggest a completely different approach,
the *Bottled Up* approach, which is based on different
principles and behaviours that are much less likely to
provoke negative feelings and behaviours from your
drinker. These approaches give you back the initiative and
power.

You might be saying "Yes, that is all very well, but I need
to keep reminding him about his drinking through these

behaviours. If I don't, then it looks as if I don't care, or, worse, I approve. In fact, he will be getting away with it!" Again, these are natural reactions. There are two answers to this, however. First, a question: has reminding him been effective in the past? Second, in the approach we will show you, you are not condoning, approving, or letting him get away with it. This new approach is just more effective and will bring a bit more peace into your life.

CHAPTER 4

The *Bottled Up* approach

So far this book has concerned itself mainly with the problems of living with a problem drinker. We have discussed the nature of alcohol problems from both medical and personal perspectives in Chapter 1. In Chapter 2 we discussed problem behaviours such as lying and denial, and in Chapter 3 we discussed how instinctive reactions not only don't work, but can actually make things worse. Now that we have laid out the problem in some detail, we want to start to introduce the alternative approach that we call *Bottled Up*. But, first, let's look at the other available approaches.

Other approaches

Although there may appear to be many programmes available, in reality they break down into three main types. The first, and probably most famous, is Al-Anon. This is the network of family groups of Alcoholics Anonymous. Al-Anon does not claim to help you motivate your partner to stop drinking; it aims to support the families and partners of drinkers. Part of its teaching is that you are powerless to change the drinker and, therefore, you need to detach from the drinker and look after yourself.

The second approach is one that has recently gained in popularity, and that is confrontation. In this approach, you are shown how to prepare for a confrontation with your drinker and how to marshal friends and relatives to support the confrontation.

The third and more recent is known by various names – for example, unilateral family therapy (UFT) or community reinforcement and family training (CRAFT). This approach teaches you various coping skills that will help to reduce your partner's drinking and motivate him to seek treatment.

All of these approaches have been shown to be successful in reducing the anxiety, helplessness, and depression in the partners of problem drinkers. They have also all demonstrated some success in motivating drinkers to stop drinking or seek treatment.

Bottled Up is a distillation of all of these approaches which is coupled with our own experience, personal and professional. Thus, in *Bottled Up* you will find advice and strategies for caring for yourself and detaching from the drinker. You will find a programme that will help you to assess the problem and to confront your drinker, but in a way that is less likely to lead to arguments and more likely to have some success. We will also show you ways of reducing your partner's motivation to drink and ways to rebuild your relationship.

Flexibility and pragmatism

One of the aspects of some self-help approaches that worries us is the apparently rigid nature of the programmes. They may leave little room for the individual to be able to express their own personality and tastes because they tend to be rather prescriptive, with members being encouraged to conform exactly to a code of conduct and behaviour. We agree that transforming a life normally requires personal changes. However, if change is to be stable, then the nature of the changes is something that needs to be chosen by the individual and not by the helping organization.

For that reason, we believe that *Bottled Up* should be viewed as a collection of guidelines and not as a rule book. Most people who read this book will have more than their fair share of guilt and shame without us adding to that burden. So we propose a positive programme that focuses on building relationships and self-esteem rather than on where people are going wrong.

Part of this approach is that we believe we need to be pragmatic or realistic in our application of the change tools. The rule-book mentality tends to lead to a situation where, regardless of the circumstances, there is little or no flexibility in how you apply the tools. Let's look at an example that you may have already met in other approaches or sources of advice.

Your partner has a heavy weekend; he has been drunk for most of it. When Monday morning arrives, he is feeling too ill to make it to work. He asks you to phone his boss and make an excuse for him. What do you do?

Almost without exception, the self-help books will tell you that you should *not* phone the boss. It is his responsibility and he needs to accept it and take the consequences. If you make the phone call, you are "enabling" him and will increase the likelihood that he will repeat this behaviour.

In principle we would agree with this advice, but it is not a rule that can be applied to everyone. What might be the possible consequences of refusing to make the phone call? Quite apart from the arguments that it may cause, there is a possibility that he could lose his job. Is that something that you could afford to happen? For example, do you have your own independent salary? If the answer to that question is yes, then by all means you should be principled and refuse to call. If, on the other hand, you do not have a lot of money and you have a couple of kids to feed, then the cost of being "principled" is considerably more and may indeed be too expensive.

We would suggest modifying the rules or principles to take personal circumstances into account. Therefore, we would say that you should not enable or cover for him, unless to do so would increase the harm you experience. So what we advocate is applying little bit of common sense to replace the rigid interpretation of the rules.

You are not powerless

Some approaches will tell you that you are powerless; that there is nothing you can do to affect whether the drinker drinks or does not drink. Obviously, this is not something that you want to hear or that is liable to give you much hope. This belief mainly arises from the twelve-step approach whose first step and fundamental principle is that "You are powerless over alcohol." The family groups (for example, Al-Anon and Alateen) also believe this. We don't!

We are not setting ourselves in opposition to the twelve-step approach as we have great respect for the whole movement. Indeed, one of us (John) got sober through AA. We even have sympathy for the principle of powerlessness as an explanation of why a problem drinker cannot control alcohol. It is just that we feel that this is a concept that is misunderstood, overstated, and therefore disempowering to drinkers and even more so to families.

There are many reasons why we don't believe in the principle of powerlessness. First is that people can and do change their drinking behaviour. Even if someone decides to become abstinent, this is a change of behaviour that is an exercise of their power. It may, as many feel, be aided by a "higher power", but that can only happen if you choose to allow that power to help you.

Another reason is that if you observe your drinker, which we are sure you do a lot, you will see that he drinks more at some times than others. Some of the times that he drinks less may be after you have had a row, or you are feeling close, or the children need him. The point is that external circumstances (and that includes you) play some part in how he behaves. This is a very important point, so let's explain it further.

Imagine that you throw a party and you invite all of the people you know who love to party. They love to dance, tell rude jokes, drink a lot, and go home around dawn. Got the picture? Now imagine you throw another party but this time you invite your parents, your boss, and all the most serious people you know. They stand around looking at their feet, struggle to make small talk, never finish their first drink and think 10 p.m. is a late night. OK, can you imagine that party? Yes, it sounds like a blast!

Now think about people's behaviour at each of the parties. Is it going to be different? You bet it's going to be different. It would probably be difficult to imagine that the different party-goers are even the same species. What about you? Is your behaviour going to be different in these situations? If so, why?

Social psychology has many theories to answer that question. It boils down to the premise that basically we are social animals and our identity (how we react or behave) varies according to the situation in which we find ourselves. Look at your role as a friend, a parent, an employee, and a partner. You would not act in the exactly the same way in all of these roles because the demands and expectations on you are different in each situation. The point is that as situations change, so too does our behaviour.

This is also true even within the same situation. For example, think about meeting your partner for the first time. Think about the first date: how you felt and how you acted. Do you still have that feeling or behave in the same way? No, because things have changed between you. You are much more familiar and secure with each other. Thus, our behaviour is influenced by the situation, the place, and the people.

Is your behaviour changing toward your partner? Do you feel that you are more distant, less loving, toward him? Is this because his behaviour has changed, because he spends more time drinking and less time with you? Is it because it is hard to believe what he says any more? You can fill in your own reasons here. The bottom line is that his change in behaviour has led to a change in your behaviour. So what do you think might happen if you changed your behaviour? Do you think that would result in him changing his behaviour?

The answer to that is yes. However, if you are going to achieve the desired effect, you need to change the right aspects of your behaviour in the right way. It is a bit like making a cake: if you don't use the correct ingredients, you can't really expect the cake you wanted. In *Bottled Up*, we will show you what to change and how to change it. We will show you how to present that change to your drinker, and how to ask for changes to his drinking in a way that is likely to be productive rather than end in a huge fight and a further rift between you. Before we start discussing the programme, let's look at our main aims for the *Bottled Up* approach.

Main aims of the *Bottled Up* approach

As we stated in the Introduction, there are six main goals underpinning this approach to living with a problem drinker. These are described below.

1. We believe that *safety/survival* is of paramount importance.

2. This approach attempts to *preserve* relationships.

3. It aims to help you to *alleviate* problems by viewing them in a more comprehensive and meaningful way.

4. It *coaches* you on how to *change* your living conditions.

5. It attempts to *empower* you to live a fulfilling life independent of his drinking.

6. It aims to help you to promote a productive *dialogue* with the drinker.

First: Safety/survival

Underpinning all of the aims needs to be your safety and survival. This is of paramount importance to us. Indeed, it is so important that it is revisited on a number of occasions and built into much of the advice we offer. We return to it again in one of the main tools of *Bottled Up*: SHARE. We understand that not all drinking relationships are physically abusive relationships. However, there are other aspects of safety that need to be examined as well. The major cause of accidents and house fires is alcohol. This is not a trivial issue.

Second: Preserve relationships

We aim to give you tools, information, and strategies that will help you to keep your relationship alive and perhaps even see it flourish. This does not mean that you will find pressure and a guilt trip if you want to end the relationship. To stay or not is, of course, a decision that each person needs to make for themselves, based on their own individual circumstances. For example, if we look at our own experience, Lou maintained her relationship even though her husband never stopped drinking, and, in John's case, his wife left him. At *Bottled Up,* we try to give you the resources to make the relationship more likely to continue.

The relationship is one of the most powerful levers for change that you have and it can bring about the desired change. Or if it does not result in change now, then, when the drinker does decide to get help or change, there will still be enough love and affection left to give you a chance of rebuilding the relationship.

Third: Alleviate problems

We will show you a practical method of addressing the extent and impact of drinking in your life. Based on the acronym HOPE, this brand-new method will give you the means to examine the main problems and tackle them in a way that is practical and effective.

Yes, of course we appreciate that your main problem is your partner's/family member's drinking and that this is causing you all sorts of grief. Using the HOPE method, however, we will show you a way of looking at your problem in a different way, a way that will allow you more control than you have at present.

We cannot guarantee that you will be problem-free or that your drinker will definitely get help or stop drinking. However, we can say that your following of the processes presented here should help to reduce your problems and make it far more likely that he will change.

Fourth: Coach and be coached

How you define a problem will determine how you tackle it. Defining your problem in a more practical and pragmatic way means that you can have options that you did not have previously.

You have tried many strategies in the past, but, almost certainly, few, if any, have worked. In *Bottled Up,* you will learn some of the strategies that don't work and why they don't, and also some strategies that may work.

Discussing change with your drinker is something that you will have tried many times. You may have had some success that was short-lived. In the main, your discussions probably included much shouting and probably tears, with little success. Sometimes you may have hit a brick wall – "I don't want to talk about it" – which, if you push it, means more shouting and tears.

We want to show you a way of approaching your drinker which will make him more likely to listen to you. It is a way that could get past the defensive wall and lead to a more productive discussion without shouting and tears. We will show you how to do this with step-by-step instructions.

Fifth: Empower

You probably spend much of your time trying to anticipate how much he will have had to drink. Can you plan an evening with friends? Is it worth cooking dinner tonight? What kind of mood will he be in when he appears?

We urge you to step out from the shadow of alcohol and start to have a life of your own. You will find pragmatic solutions to difficult issues that should give you more freedom to pursue your own goals.

Our aim is to empower you to take back control of your life. We want you to enjoy your life and not endure his. As a side effect, when the power balance shifts (which is one of our aims), then often healing can happen for individuals and for relationships.

Sixth: Promote dialogue

If any progress is going to be made, it will require that both the partner and the drinker enter into a dialogue about the effect of the drinking. We will show you how that can be accomplished and the way to approach this dialogue when we discuss LOVE and SHARE.

If you want your drinker to change his drinking or seek help, then you need to be able to discuss the issues in an amicable manner. We will show you how to approach the issues in a way that is more likely to result in a positive outcome.

These, then, are the overall goals and philosophy of *Bottled Up*. It is a philosophy that will promote the positives in your life while trying to reduce the negatives. Even if you are not be able to change his drinking (although if you follow this programme, we think you will), you can still reduce the effect it has on your life and actively pursue a happy and fulfilling life. In this book we will introduce you to the tools to accomplish this. In the following chapters we will show you how to use the process we call HOPE and the tool we call SHARE, and adopt the attitude we call LOVE. All of these (HOPE, SHARE, and LOVE) are acronyms for the powerful approach that *Bottled Up* will show you. It is an approach that, quite literally, could change your life.

CHAPTER 5

HOPE

In this chapter we introduce the process we call HOPE. Like many useful things in life, it is quite simple but very powerful if properly applied. Of course, reading this book will not solve your problems any more than reading a fitness book will build muscle or reading a diet book will result in weight loss. The results in all these cases come from applying the lessons learned within the books. If you apply the principles laid out in this book, you will see changes in your life.

To achieve the change that you hope for requires preparation and work. You need a plan to follow. A common saying in motivational talks is "Fail to plan and plan to fail." There is some truth in that. We understand that many of you may find the journey that you are travelling on exhausting, so we have tried to make these steps as easy as possible. We suggest that you take your time and tackle what you can when you can.

Almost certainly, you have had no real idea of what you want changed and how. OK, you want him to stop or cut down his drinking, but how is this going to happen and what are the expected outcomes?

In *Bottled Up,* we offer you a clear step-by-step

programme to help you achieve the changes that you want. The first part of the programme is HOPE. However, before we look at HOPE, let's look at a bit of psychology.

You have probably been looking for a way to control his drinking or to get him to admit he is an alcoholic and seek help from the family doctor, join AA, or go into rehab. Almost certainly, you have exhausted every idea of how to do that. You have attempted some or all of the strategies we have mentioned: used logic, appealed to his better nature, pleaded, threatened, sulked, thrown tantrums, had blazing rows, left, threatened to leave... You saw change for a short time, or promises that were made, broken, remade, rebroken. The bottom line is that nothing has worked. If it had worked, you would not be reading this – there would be no reason to. We want to show you another way: a possible solution to your dilemma. First, the psychology.

Learned helplessness

A well-respected psychologist, Martin Seligman, carried out a number of experiments with dogs. He placed them in a situation where they were given electric shocks, with no possibility of escape (they were chained in place). Later, he gave them shocks again, but this time they could escape (the chains were removed). However, even though the chains had been removed, many of them did not even try to escape. They tended to remain where they were and accept the shocks. He called this state learned helplessness.

Seligman and his colleagues later investigated this learned helplessness in humans and found similar patterns of behaviour. It is a condition that is found particularly in people in war zones and hostage victims. The resulting research concluded, first, that people become depressed when they think that they no longer have control over their lives, and, second, that they hold themselves responsible for this helpless state. The condition can lead to depression, feelings of extreme stress, and health problems.

Other research has found that not everyone who is subjected to difficult, uncontrollable situations shows signs of learned helplessness to the same degree or, indeed, at all. Some people appear to be resistant. What has been discovered to be important is how the person views the situation. If they feel that they are powerless to change the situation, they develop learned helplessness; if they feel that they have power to control or alter the situation, they don't develop it or develop it to a lesser degree. Further research has shown that learned helplessness can be prevented and/or reversed. Again, the view of the situation and the perception of having even a little control were the main factors that made the difference. Teaching people to view a situation in a different way can make a great difference.

So what has this got to do with you and living with a problem drinker? You are not a hostage, being given electric shocks, or living in a war zone, although sometimes it may seem like it! In the next section we will explore how a knowledge of learned helplessness and strategies to overcome it might help you in your situation.

Learned helplessness and living with a problem drinker

As we stated above, the main features of learned helplessness (LH) are that there is a difficult and sometimes dangerous situation, and a feeling that one has no control over the situation. Living with a problem drinker is very often a difficult and sometimes dangerous situation because his behaviour can be abusive and disruptive, and it certainly induces stress. As you have found to your cost, you have little or no control over that behaviour. That being the case, you probably feel depressed (or at least despairing) and stressed, and your health may be suffering. (We will explore these consequences more in Chapter 7 – SHARE. There is, however, something that you can do about it.

First, change the way you view the situation.

Second, gain some control.

Tackling learned helplessness

First, change how you view the situation. You may think that this is difficult. After all, how else can you view it? He gets drunk and you're miserable, or he is always drinking and you never know what he is going to do next. OK, fair enough, they are the facts, but what does need to change is your view of what can be done about it.

Until now, you have probably been looking for the perfect words, the perfect time to say them, and the perfect way to say them. If you can just do that, then everything will change! He will see the error of his ways. He will stop drinking, go into rehab, and you will have the man that you fell in love with back in your life and can move on to a happy ever after. Right? Well, actually, no. Wrong!

It is unlikely that the right words or any combination of time, tone, or any other circumstance is going to be the prime mover in causing change. In other words, it is unlikely that you will change his drinking in this way. Not the words that you hoped to read, but these may be the words that set you free. We discussed this in Chapter 3, but it is so important that we will say it again. *You are unlikely to change his drinking in this way!*

Continuing to believe that you can and continuing to try to do so is a road that leads to misery, disappointment, and learned helplessness. There is an old saying: "Madness is doing the same thing over and over and expecting a different result". Are you doing that?

So what can you do? That is where HOPE comes in. This is a new way of looking at the situation and a way of gaining some control over it. That control should save you from developing learned helplessness or start to reverse it if it has already set in.

What the *Bottled Up* approach does is focus not on what you can't change but instead on what you can change. *Bottled Up* gives you tools and a strategy to use them that can bring about changes in your life.

Let us start by introducing you to HOPE.

HOPE stands for:

Assess the **Harm**

Survey the **Options**

Promote change

Evaluate your progress

This is a process that should be carried out in sequence (see the diagram). First, assess the harm; second, survey the options; third, promote change; fourth, evaluate your progress. If you have achieved the desired effect, then stop. If not, continue round the process again.

The elements of HOPE are explained below.

Assess the Harm

You may not think that you need to carry out an assessment of the harm that alcohol is doing in your life. After all, you have lived with it and it has caused severe disruption, heartache, and pain in your home, so you know the problems only too well. We would certainly not suggest that you are unaware of the problems; however, we would argue that you *do* need to make an assessment of them.

Until now, you have almost certainly never taken a systematic look at the role of alcohol in your life. Yes, you will be very aware of *some* of the problems that it causes, but you will be much less aware of others. The most common comment people make after carrying out the assessment is that they had not realized how much alcohol had affected their lives.

The process of HOPE requires you to carry out a systematic assessment. The reason for this is to help you to look at the problems in a structured and unemotional way. The assessment will give you a better idea of what you can and can't change, and will lead to an array of options about how you deal with the issues. To carry out the assessment, we will introduce you to a tool that will help you focus on all aspects of your life. That tool is SHARE and we will lead you through its use in later pages.

Survey the Options

For any problem, there are several possible options that can be applied. Generally, the option chosen depends on a number of factors. It would obviously depend on the nature of the problem, the severity of the problem, the urgency for a resolution, what you are capable of doing, and what is actually acceptable to you.

We believe in the need to be realistic, rather than prescriptive. We don't believe that there are any set solutions that can be trotted out any time a particular problem arises. That is a dangerous and superficial approach that is at odds with the *Bottled Up* approach encapsulated in the goals presented in Chapter 4.

There are two main options available – SHARE and LOVE – that we will introduce over the next few chapters. It is important to note that they are not mutually exclusive; selecting one does not mean rejecting the other. These two tools are complementary and could be used together quite easily.

SHARE, as well as being the main instrument of assessment, is also a way of reducing the harm that is being caused by alcohol. It is aimed not at controlling drinking but rather at controlling the *consequences* of alcohol. This is a good tool to use to begin regaining some control in your life. It is also a strategy that is better suited for the heavier drinker who has been drinking problematically for years.

Some aspects of LOVE are probably better suited to cases where the drinking pattern is less established or the drinking is not so heavy. This is not to say that they will not have an effect on your long-term heavy drinker. It is just that it may be better to begin with SHARE and introduce some of the aspects of LOVE at a later stage.

If this sounds complicated, don't worry; we will talk you through which tool to use, how, and when.

Promote change

In this part of the cycle, you will start to promote change. Before describing how you bring about change, let's have a look at how and why people change.

Generally, people change for two reasons: to avoid bad things (for example, punishment) or to get good things (a reward). For most of us it is not as simple as one reason or the other; it is usually a combination of both. Drinkers are no different. They also change for good or bad things or a combination of both.

The most common, or stereotypical, picture we have of a drinker changing is that he continues drinking until he hits rock bottom. Then, and only then, will he do something about his drinking. There is evidence that suggests there is some truth to this picture – that people change when the consequences of drinking alcohol get bad. However, what actually constitutes "rock bottom" is very different for each person. For some it may be that they lose everything, but for others rock bottom is a much less extreme place. It could mean that rather than having lost their family, they have instead lost love or respect, or instead of being extremely physically ill, they have had a health scare. The principle is the same. They may still be changing because of negative outcomes, but the outcomes tend to be less severe.

Recent research has suggested that a concept called social capital is both an important factor in change and a protective factor against incurring too much harm. Social capital can be viewed as a measure of how much support someone has. For example, someone who is married, has a family, a job, and lots of friends has far more social capital than someone who is single, jobless, and friendless. It has been found that those who have high social capital have a higher level of rock bottom and tend to recover from alcohol problems more quickly and with greater stability. The other way of looking at social capital is that it has a protective factor because people with high social capital have more to lose.

The second common reason for change is to get something better. We often use rewards to get people to change. Society runs on this principle; we call it economics. I pay you £x and you do something for me.

Both the good and the bad feature in change. For example, many people give up smoking because of health reasons, but those same people may not go back for positive reasons – feeling fitter, smelling nicer, and so on. *Bottled Up* makes use of both negative and positive reasons for change. This is especially true of LOVE.

In *Bottled Up*, you will be shown how to detach so that the drinker can experience the naturally occurring negative consequences of alcohol – the bad things. You will also be shown how to entice change, through offering good things. Thus you will be using some of his social capital (you, his family, and his friends) to help your drinker change and stay changed.

The initial goal of the change is *not* to get him to stop drinking, or even to cut down his drinking, although it is entirely possible that these may be the indirect effects of your actions. The initial focus of your change is to make your home and your life safer and more comfortable for your family and yourself.

Some of these changes may mean setting boundaries and negotiating limits. We will discuss these issues in much more detail at the appropriate point.

The second goal of change is for you to detach from your drinker's behaviour and start living a life that is not focused on or dependent on his behaviour. We want to show you how to live in a way that is more proactive than reactive.

The final change is (if at all possible) to start to repair your relationship. We will show you how to rekindle some of the love and common interests that attracted you to each other.

All of these strategies and tools will be introduced in the next few chapters. In these chapters you will find flexible tools that you can tailor to your own situation. You will also find that, in trying to make changes in your life, we recommend multiple approaches, not just a single strategy. This multi-faceted change process is closer to what happens naturally. What we are suggesting may accelerate the process and save your own sanity.

Evaluate your progress

To know whether your strategies are working and if your circumstances are improving, you will need to carry out an evaluation. This will mean comparing where you are now with how you were when you carried out the SHARE assessment.

Possible outcomes are that things have improved, in which case your strategies are working and you should keep doing what you are doing, or things may be much the same or even worse, in which case you need to rethink what you are doing.

Another (not uncommon) outcome is that things are much the same but *you* have improved. Having a perception of control over the situation can make a huge difference.

In the next two chapters we will introduce LOVE and SHARE. We will then return to HOPE in Chapter 8 where we will show you how to use this model.

CHAPTER 6

LOVE

LOVE was one of the first elements of the *Bottled Up* approach. When we talked about how change could be promoted, we felt that a positive approach that persuades was better than one that bullied or used browbeating tactics. As we talked about how we ourselves had changed, how we had helped others change, and what the research said, we increasingly felt that a "softer" approach would be more effective; one that coaxed and persuaded was what appeared to work.

For some of you reading this book, this may seem completely contrary to what you believe, particularly with regards to your drinker. As we have said in other chapters (especially Chapter 3), that is a completely understandable and natural reaction. However, if you do want your circumstances to change for the better, then it is time to learn and apply new behaviours.

Ask yourself: which do you respond better to – a smile or a frown, an encouraging word or a rebuke? LOVE works on that principle. However, it is not just a way of convincing someone to change by being nice to them. It is one of the fundamental principles of social psychology. We will explain this further later in the chapter, but, first, what do we mean by LOVE, and why is it in capital letters?

What do we mean by LOVE?

LOVE is another acronym. We use it to remember and highlight a process that *may* encourage change in your drinker but will *definitely* encourage change in yourself and family life.

LOVE stands for:

Let the drinker experience the negative consequences of drinking.

Optimize your time together when the drinker is sober.

Value the drinker as the person you love(d).

Encourage change.

It was no accident that we chose LOVE as our acronym. We chose it, obviously, because it fitted what we see as the important elements for change, but also because it was so different from the most common reactions to living with a problem drinker, such as anger and a desire to punish.

We view LOVE not just as a feeling but as a way of behaving. Indeed, many people have said that love is about action rather than emotion. One of the most common Bible readings at weddings is from Paul's first letter to the Corinthians (Chapter 13), where he says:

> *Love is patient, love is kind. It does not envy, it*
> *does not boast, it is not proud. It is not rude, it is*

*not self-seeking, it is not easily angered, it keeps
no record of wrongs. Love does not delight in evil
but rejoices with the truth. It always protects,
always trusts, always hopes, always perseveres.
Love never fails.*

You are probably saying "Yeah, this sounds great when you are getting married and everything seems perfect, but afterwards it seems like a tall order!" This may be true, but it is nevertheless an interesting definition. It lifts our ideas of love from being a feeling that gives us a silly look on our face to a code for behaving. An example of this in action can be seen in a mother looking at her newborn child with goo-goo eyes. It is a lovely sight, but the child won't survive long with just soppy looks. It needs the mother to care for it, feed it, change it, and keep it safe. Love makes us want to care for, to protect, and to tend to the welfare of the object of our love – these are the actions of love.

LOVE is at the heart of the *Bottled Up* approach. It is the foundation of change for you and your drinker. It is a way that helps to create closeness rather than distance. It can reawaken feelings that you may not have experienced for some time. It can reintroduce into your life the enjoyment of shared interests and can bring joy to replace the misery that you have felt and may feel now.

LOVE is not a soft option for you or the drinker. It is not you condoning or colluding in his drinking behaviour. It is not "letting him get away with it", as people have often suggested to us. It is a challenging way to behave because it means learning entirely new actions and reactions.

Reading this book will not make your problems disappear. This book is a blueprint for change, but only if you put the suggestions into action. Even if you do put the lessons in this book into action, it is unlikely that your circumstances will change overnight. Change takes time and persistence. Change takes work. If you are ready to put that work in, then we will show you how you can alter your life.

First of all, the key to change in your life lies with *you*. The most likely way that your drinker is going to change his drinking behaviour is if you change yours.

After reading this, you may be thinking "If I need to change my behaviour, does that mean that it is my fault?" Absolutely not! You have probably been trying to control or contain the drinking behaviour for many years. You have been using the various tools that you have learned both in your childhood and over the years of living with a drinker. Generally, these tools would be punishing, picking a fight, policing, and pleading (look at Chapter 3). In most circumstances, these tools would have an effect. But not here!

So you need a new approach. Like most people in your position, you have been trying to accomplish a job with the wrong tools. This is not about guilt. It is about being better equipped. We want to equip you now, to give you the right tools this time. Please be clear: these are tools that are designed to change your circumstances and your drinker. They are not the result of some political correctness agenda or airy-fairy ideas, nor are they some sort of morality code detailing how we feel you should behave. They are techniques grounded in science, research, and experience. In Chapter 8 we will show you step-by-step how to use these tools, but first we will introduce the rationale that underpins them.

Let the drinker experience the negative consequences of drinking

Watching someone struggle or suffer is difficult for most people. When that person is someone you love, then the difficulty is increased enormously and it would seem to run completely contrary to our discussion of LOVE above. However, protecting your loved one from any or all negative outcomes means that they do not learn the consequences of their actions. For example, what would happen if every time your daughter went shopping, she overspent and you paid her credit card bill every month? She would never learn to budget and, in the long run, you would not be helping her.

It is often through our mistakes, struggles, and suffering that we learn. The drinker is the same. If you always make excuses for him, make sure that he is not inconvenienced, then why should he change? There is no incentive to alter his behaviour. If you make it clear that when he chooses to drink, any consequences are his responsibility and that you are no longer covering for him, clearing up after him, or protecting him, then he will start to feel the effects of his drinking and it will become less attractive.

Look at the example we gave of the spendthrift daughter. How might she react if she was left to pay her own bills? She might behave differently on the next shopping trip, or it might take a few times of her being in debt before she learned. Sometimes things get worse before they get better. The drinker is the same. If you are always making excuses to friends, keeping the kids from seeing their dad drunk, or clearing up after him, then, like the overspending daughter, he does not need to "pay" for his drinking or feel the consequences.

This is not about punishment; this is about him taking responsibility for his own choices. That is a very important point. You are not doing it to him; he is doing it to himself.

What happens at the moment in your house? Do you stay up to make sure your drinker makes it to bed? Do you make sure his clothes are clean and put away? Do you keep food warm for him if he is late home because he stopped for a drink? Do you make sure the kids are quiet on a Sunday morning because Dad is "not feeling very well" (we know he has a raging hangover)? Do you make excuses to his friends when he lets them down? Have you given up asking Dad for a lift anywhere? Do you avoid meeting your friends at your house or having them stay over?

If you are doing all or even any of these things, then *you* are the one who is experiencing the negatives consequences of his drinking – not him. Why should he change? It is not causing him a problem; it is causing *you* a problem! It is time to stop shielding him. Let him take the consequences of his actions.

If he doesn't make it to bed, let him sleep on the floor. If his clothes are dirty or not put away, that's his problem, not yours. If he doesn't make it on time for the meal you cooked, throw it away and let him cook for himself. If the kids are noisy, let them be. Why should they suffer for his drinking? Stop making excuses to his friends – they probably know what is going on anyway.

Be wise

This is not an idea that is exclusive to *Bottled Up*. Most agencies that give advice about living with a problem drinker will give similar advice. *Bottled Up* differs in two respects. First, some of these other agencies suggest that you cannot change the drinker; we disagree – you can. The second difference is that we offer some pragmatic guidelines to help your decision.

Although we suggest that you should not intervene and so let the drinker experience the negatives, do not stand back if the drinker is in actual physical danger.

As discussed in Chapter 4, if alcohol is affecting his ability to work, many experts will tell you not to phone the boss and make excuses. However, when you make that decision, you need to consider the family income and how you would pay bills if he lost his job. If you are the main breadwinner or have an independent income, then that advice may be fine; otherwise, be realistic in your judgment.

In short, you should allow him to experience the negative consequences of his drinking as long as it does not put him, your family, or you in direct danger.

You may find it difficult or feel guilty about standing back, particularly if you have protected him for many years. There is no need to feel this way. Remember, it is his choice, not yours! You are choosing to detach and let him make his own choices and clean up his own mess.

You might be asking "What happened to Paul the apostle and his views on love? Have we just abandoned them?" No, we haven't. Unfortunately, some things that are done in the name of love are ill-conceived. Even if we are acting in a loving manner, we need to take a more long-term view. You would almost certainly not attempt to withhold a reward if your partner earned it. You would not take that reward for yourself, so why should you take the negative consequences?

All the research shows that the negative consequences are what teaches the drinker about the harm of drinking and helps him change. Therefore, shielding him – by taking that harm on yourself – prevents him learning and is actually harming him. Protecting him may actually prolong his drinking career; letting him experience the consequences may shorten his drinking career and be the true loving act.

There is another aspect to this. If you stop clearing up after him and waiting around for him to come home, stop drinking, sober up, or whatever, you will have some time to yourself. While he continues to drink, use that time to do something for you. Find something that interests you. Perhaps you have always wanted to learn a new skill or take a course. Now is the time to do it. Have you been avoiding friends because you felt ashamed of his drinking? Well, don't. Spend time with friends and talk freely – you are no longer protecting him, remember? Let your friends support you. They almost certainly know what is going on already, so it may be a relief for everybody if you talk openly. Chapter 9 discusses these issues in more detail.

Optimize your time together when the drinker is sober

If you felt uncomfortable with the previous section, you may feel more comfortable with this next aspect of LOVE. In this part, the purpose is to bring the fun and togetherness back into your life. Although leaving him to experience the negatives should encourage change, it is also true that the drinker is more likely to be persuaded to change his drinking behaviour if there is a positive incentive; that is, if there is a better alternative on offer. This is not a feature of alcoholism; it is a feature of human beings that they are more likely to change if there is a reward involved rather than a sacrifice. Besides, you deserve a bit of fun as well.

There are two motives to the rationale behind this part of the strategy. The first is to foster a closeness between you and your drinker. The second is to present your drinker with a barrier to his drinking.

You have probably felt that for some time there has been some distance between you. His behaviour – getting drunk, lying, being undependable – leaves you seething and resentful. You long for the days when you were close and these problems did not exist, but you know that until he changes his behaviour it is not possible.

This is where it becomes difficult for you. This is where you need to change your behaviour and your attitude. A great part of your brain will be screaming at you "You can't even think of rewarding him till he changes!" However, if you want change to happen, you need to take a different outlook. If you want to be close, then someone needs to create the circumstances for it to happen. At the moment, that someone is going to have to be you. You need to be the mature one and take the lead.

So start thinking about what you like to do together that does not involve drinking? It may be some time since you did these things, but try to remember things that you both enjoy. One purpose of this exercise is to offer alternatives to drinking, so make sure that it is something your drinker actually likes and would consider a treat. Examples might be walking in the country or on a beach, a trip to the cinema or theatre or a concert, a romantic night in. Try to think of as many things as you can that the drinker would enjoy. You are trying to put obstacles in the way of his drinking by offering him an alternative. Make sure it is something that you would enjoy as well; otherwise, you could end up doing things that make you miserable and that would defeat the purpose. You are trying to show him that it is a lot more fun spending time with you than drinking.

By offering alternatives to drinking, you are doing a number of things. First, you are showing him that life could be good if he was not drinking. It does not need to be dull and boring, but instead would be much more varied, and you could rekindle the spark between you. Second, you are showing him that you want to be with him, that you want to share your life with him and have fun. Third, you are making it clear that he does have a choice and it is his responsibility if he chooses the drinking option.

Value the drinker as the person you love(d)

Having read this far, you probably have rather mixed emotions. The idea of letting go and letting him experience the negative consequences of his drinking probably brought up all your negative emotions – fear, anger, outrage, disappointment, and frustration. Then the optimizing stage probably brought the joy of remembering things you did together, tinged with sadness that you don't do these things any more. These are all natural emotions and it would be surprising if you did not feel emotional and confused.

At some stage, when you put the *Bottled Up* approach

into action, you are going to organize a discussion with your drinker. Your emotional state may be crucial to this discussion. If you go into it angry, the result may be an argument, but if you approach it in a loving and caring manner, the result could be very positive. Remember what psychologists call "the self-fulfilling prophecy", which says that if you think a person is worthless (or worthy), they often behave in a way that is consistent with your beliefs. The point is that they pick up your beliefs about them and act accordingly. So focus on the good qualities and that may reignite positive feelings in both of you.

Unfortunately, one of the first casualties of a relationship where there is a drinker is respect. The frequent lies and undependability mean that the respect you had for the person might be eroded and then disappear altogether. You stop believing just about anything he says, especially if it concerns drinking. You may start to feel contempt for him – and may even show it.

Alcohol is very destructive in a relationship. Just as paint-stripper removes the shine from a table top, so alcohol can remove the gloss from a relationship. In this part of the LOVE strategy, we try to redress that balance by rekindling the love that you once felt (and perhaps still do feel) for each other.

Valuing your drinker fits nicely with optimizing your time together. Part of remembering what you enjoyed doing together will evoke good memories of what he was like before the drinking. What was it that attracted you to each other? Try to remember what he was like then – how you talked, laughed, what you did, how you felt. Things may have changed, perhaps drastically. However, if you can rekindle the flame of love, then maybe you will discover that he, and your relationship, is worth fighting for.

Encourage change

This is the last part of the LOVE approach. It has two aspects to it. The first is to encourage and support any move toward change, such as a visit to a doctor or rehab, or even a less dramatic move, such as a reduction in the amount of consumption. You have probably seen and heard the promises and gestures before, but do be encouraging. Research has found that successfully changing any addiction, such as alcohol or smoking, usually takes a few attempts. So each attempt is one closer to actually changing.

The second aspect of encouraging change is to do what is suggested above. Let him experience the negatives. We do realize that this is difficult and that it means breaking old habits, but it is essential; otherwise, you may actually be preventing him from changing. Optimize your time with him by planning great tempting alternatives to drinking. Value him by remembering why you were attracted to him and what you are fighting for.

When you carry out the behaviours described in LOVE, they may seem awkward and contrived in the beginning. With practice, they will become more natural. To begin with, you may be filled with negative emotions and you may need to address these first. (Chapter 13 discusses the emotional rollercoaster.)

To recap, LOVE is an action, or a series of actions. These actions are designed to bring change to your circumstances. However, it is important to remember that LOVE (or any programme) will not bring change unless you apply its principles and keep applying them. But if you do that, then the rewards could be very worthwhile.

CHAPTER 7

SHARE

In Chapter 1 we talked about how you know whether your drinker has an alcohol problem. Although we gave you the clinical criteria from *DSM-IV*, we suggested that it is less about whether he has a diagnosable problem and more about whether his drinking is causing a problem in your life and relationship. In this chapter we will take that a bit further and show you a method that allows you to make your own assessment of the problem in a way that can be used to *change* the problem. This method is called SHARE.

SHARE is a new way of looking at your situation of living with a problem drinker. As you have probably found out from bitter experience, focusing on the drinking behaviour has not been very productive. You have probably been met with one of two reactions (or maybe both): downright denial that there is a problem or promises to change that are constantly broken, renewed, and rebroken.

As we discussed in Chapter 1, one of the many problems of addressing the drinking directly is the question of definitions. You very quickly get into the territory of how much is too much. He always knows someone, lots of people even, who drink far more than him. He may even name a few. How you are going to check the accuracy of that statement is a mystery, but it is often a closing statement that, translated, means "Lots of people drink more than me; now leave me alone." The other definition problem is the word "alcoholic". This is an emotive word and all drinkers believe they know the definition of it. In their minds, the definition of an alcoholic is, in a nutshell, "someone who is not me". Few people want to admit to being different in any way from their peers, and being an alcoholic seems to carry one of the largest stigmas there is. So they will find any reason to not be labelled an alcoholic. "Alcoholics drink every day and I don't. Alcoholics are always drunk and I'm not." Arguing with someone about their drinking is usually a fruitless task and a waste of time.

What SHARE does instead is have you focus on the actual effect that the drinker is having on your life. That way, instead of worrying about the drinking behaviour (how much he drinks and whether that makes him an alcoholic, dependent drinker, or binge drinker), you focus on the consequences. By doing that, you can see whether and in what way his drinking threatens your quality of life, your relationships, or your health.

SHARE is not a ticklist that will give you a meaningless score at the end. This is a purposeful and personal look at, and assessment of, *your* circumstances. It is a powerful tool to give you a clearer picture of your situation and what you can do about it. It is not difficult; however, it does require you to take time and put effort into it. Like most things in life, the more time and effort you put in, the more you will gain. This is probably the first time you have examined your life and circumstances in such detail and with such purpose.

One of the reasons for examining his drinking in this way is that the arguments about whether he drinks too much and what is too much, whether he is an alcoholic and what is an alcoholic, just don't arise. Those questions are irrelevant because when you talk to him later you will discuss the effects of his drinking on you and your family.

We need to warn you at this stage that carrying out the SHARE assessment can have an emotional impact. We suggest you ensure that you have someone close to give you support if you need it.

SHARE

SHARE is another acronym. This one is a shorthand method of describing the areas of our lives that can be affected by the behaviour of a drinker. These are as follows:

Safety

Health

Ambition

Relationships

Environment

Safety

The first and most important area of your life that may be affected by drinking is your safety. It is possible that he is violent and aggressive when he is drinking. So you may fear that you or your family will be physically assaulted. Alternatively, you may feel that although he has never been violent in the past, he is very aggressive verbally and you are frightened. Clearly, this is a situation that cannot be ignored. If there is violence and aggression, then we suggest that you ensure that you, your children, and anyone else who lives with you are safe.

As you read in Chapter 4, one of our goals for the *Bottled Up* approach is to preserve and enhance relationships, so we do not give this advice lightly. We also said that we did not believe in rules. However, when there is violence involved, you should give very serious thought to whether you should remain in the relationship, or at least in the same house.[1] If you do decide to stay, then take some precautions. Keep a mobile phone handy and programme the police and a friend on speed dial. Ask a friend or relative to provide a bed for you, and your children if you have any, on the nights he is drinking heavily. You might want to pack a suitcase with clothes for a few days and leave it at your friend's house. Make sure that they know and understand the problem. The more people who know of the potential for violence, the safer you become. This is not a time to hide the problems you are facing.

Even if he is not aggressive or violent, and many drinkers are not, you may still fear for your safety. He may smoke while drinking and you fear that he will fall asleep and start a fire.

---

1 Although it is the ethos of this programme to preserve relationships, please note that if any of these things are happening we strongly suggest that you consult your doctor and/or your solicitor:

- *your partner is physically and/or sexually assaulting you*
- *your partner is physically and/or sexually assaulting your children*
- *you feel that your physical or mental health are severely at risk.*

Or he may be hungry when drunk and cook late at night when you are asleep. He may drive when drinking, perhaps taking the children with him. When drunk, he may bring home people you would rather not have in your house. He may go out and leave the doors unlocked or the windows open. There are many reasons that you may worry about your safety that are directly attributable to drinking.

We will look at some of the more common problems and suggest possible solutions in Chapter 9.

Health

Since he is the one who is drinking, he may say "Well, who am I hurting? Only me." This is not actually true. You may find that your health is suffering, and suffering badly, through his drinking.

You may find that your level of anxiety is high, that you can't sleep or eat. Or you may find that you are depressed and that you are tired and sleepy much of the time. You may be eating for comfort or you may have no appetite and don't eat very much, and therefore your weight may be increasing rapidly or dropping off. You may have high levels of irritability, sadness for no apparent reason, and mood swings, all of which can be linked to the uncertainty inherent in living with a drinker. Your self-esteem is probably suffering and you feel indecisive and unsure of yourself, and this can exacerbate all of the problems listed above.

You may find that you have more colds, infections, or rashes. Or you may find that you do not recover from seasonal illnesses as easily or quickly as you once did. You may just feel tired, run down, listless, and generally unwell.

All of these symptoms are common in people who

live with a problem drinker. The stress of living with the uncertainty of whether the drinker is going to get drunk or stay sober is very difficult to handle. In fact, stress is more common in situations where there is uncertainty than in situations where there is a certainty of a negative event, such as imminent bereavement.

So if he says "I'm only hurting myself", then clearly this is untrue.

Ambition

This area of your life is much more difficult to quantify, but it is possibly one of the most important of all. We all have dreams, ambitions, and aspirations, both as individuals and, if applicable, as a family. These dreams and aspirations can be affected and even shattered by alcohol. The shared dreams of what your marriage would be like are common casualties of drinking. So too are your dreams for your children.

Your ambitions may involve money, possessions, a bigger house, clothes, a car, holidays. As we know, drinking can seriously affect earning power. Jobs can be lost through poor performance, absenteeism, or disruptive behaviour. Promotions or career advancements can be closed to a drinker, who can then become more resentful as he sees "inferior" colleagues promoted over him.

Even if you have a regular income, it can be frittered away on alcohol. It can take a considerable amount of money to sustain heavy drinking, and that cost competes with any other channels for your money or ambitions you may have.

However, your ambitions and dreams may be much

less tangible than money, status, or power. They may be a reflection of what you thought would make you happy. It may be a lifestyle that centred round a family, togetherness, and love. It may have included qualities such as honesty, trust, and respect.

This is one area that is very personal. Our dreams and ambitions are as diverse as we are. Only you know what your ambitions are or were and how alcohol has affected them.

Relationships

Unfortunately, relationships are frequent victims of heavy drinking. As the drinking increases, all relationships – marriages or partnerships, relationships with children, siblings, parents, and friends – often suffer. And, as he drinks more and his behaviour becomes more unpredictable, you probably find yourself withdrawing from the very people who might help you most – your friends.

Embarrassment, shame, and guilt may stop you talking to your friends. As you try harder to cover up his drinking, it becomes harder to face your friends and lie to them, telling them everything is OK.

If the drinker is your partner, husband or wife, then the biggest casualty of the drinking may be this primary relationship. You probably find your feelings of love, respect, and pride evaporating. Sometimes they may be replaced by contempt, fear, loathing, distrust, even hate. You may feel guilty about these negative feelings, even try to process them healthily, but, in the end, you may feel overwhelmed by the frequency of his failures. You end up powerless to do anything about it as the relationship suffers.

Environment

Your environment is your immediate surroundings, your home. Do you feel that this is suffering due to his drinking? Is the fabric of the home suffering? For example, has hygiene deteriorated? Have repairs not been done or old worn-out items not been replaced? Is the home being damaged carelessly or wilfully?

Are things being broken or damaged when he is drinking and angry? Are the furniture and carpets being burned by having cigarettes dropped on them?

Do you feel ashamed that the exterior of the house has not been painted or repaired? Has the garden been tidied and the grass cut, or has it been left to grow wild?

Your home should be the place where you feel peaceful and safe. Does your home have a sense of peace and safety? Do you feel happy to invite people into your home when they call, or do you dread visitors because you feel embarrassed about the state of the house? Is your home somewhere people like to visit?

When you carry out the SHARE assessment, you will have a much clearer picture of where alcohol is causing problems in your life and what those problems are. This information can be used to assess the extent of your problems and it can also be used to help reduce those problems.

We don't expect that everyone will have problems in all of the SHARE areas, or have them all to the same degree. Some of you may be in the early days of your relationship and that may be the area that is suffering most. Others may have been experiencing problems for many years and have problems in all areas of your life. As we have already acknowledged, you are all individuals with different expectations, different experiences, and different problems. We believe that any programme must recognize this and be flexible enough to apply to very diverse situations. We have tried to ensure that *Bottled Up* has that flexibility.

In the next chapters we will show you how to use SHARE as a tool to assess your situation, starting with an assessment of your safety.

CHAPTER 8

HOPE in action: Assess the harm

We have now introduced you to the three major elements of *Bottled Up* – HOPE, SHARE, and LOVE – and the rationale that underpins them. In this chapter, we are going to show you how you can put them together to try to create change in your life and home.

This book has two tasks. One is to help you change your drinker's behaviour. The other is to help you to change how you react to and interact with your drinker. The most important factor in being successful in the first of these tasks is achieving the second. That is, if you manage to change your own behaviour, then you have a greater chance of changing your drinker's. We are sure that you feel impatient to start and for change to happen. Nevertheless, we urge you to give yourself time to follow these steps as they are laid out here, even if you do feel impatient. Don't skip or jump over steps. They are designed this way for a reason.

We also urge you to take a break between assessments and meetings. Some of these exercises may awaken feelings and emotions that have been buried or suppressed

– maybe even for years – and you need time to process these feelings. For this approach to be successful, you need to approach your drinker, at best, in a warm and loving way or, at worst, with a detached and unemotional manner. If you have strong, seething, negative emotions coursing through you, this will be difficult to achieve. So give yourself time to complete the assessment and time to absorb the information and the accompanying emotion.

Before starting this section we need to set a few other principles:

- Safety is paramount; do not put yourself at risk.

- The more work you put into the preparation, the more likely that you will have a good outcome.

- It is unlikely that change will happen immediately. You will almost certainly need to repeat these tasks a number of times before you achieve the desired effect.

- Have patience. Problems generally take time to establish and so they also take time to change.

In order to provide a framework to create change, we are going to follow the HOPE process and also incorporate the assessments from SHARE and LOVE. As stated in Chapter 5, harm is the first element of the HOPE acronym, so we will start by assessing the harm.

Assessing the harm
Part 1

In this first exercise you will make a thorough assessment of the impact of drinking on the important areas of your life. This will give you a clearer view of the problem. Remember that there are no right or wrong answers to this assessment; there are no diagnoses dependent on what you say. It is important to remember that this is purely and simply your view of your life as it is affected by alcohol. As we discussed in Chapter 1, you don't need anyone to tell you whether you have a problem or not – you know that yourself. After all, you are the one who lives it. So include anything that is a problem for you or your family, regardless of what you believe others may think about it.

For this and the other assessments, get a pen and paper. You may also find a highlighter pen useful. You may want to have a notebook or a folder especially for these exercises as you will want to refer to this and other assessments at a later date. Choose a quiet place where you will not be disturbed, switch off your phone, and remove any distractions. You will probably want complete privacy for this exercise, as you may find that you stir up some mixed emotions.

Don't be surprised if you find yourself feeling angry, sad, frustrated, fearful, or any other deep and powerful emotion. This is to be expected. This exercise is almost certainly the first time that you have looked at the true effects of drinking on your life in this kind of detail. You are likely to awaken many feelings and emotions that you have ignored, denied, or suppressed over months and years. Thus, the result could be a strong release of feelings – what psychologists would call a catharsis. You have almost certainly bottled up your feelings about drinking, so this reaction could be strong. Don't worry about it. It is normal, even if it is painful. On the other hand, you may have few or no feelings awakened by this process. Again, don't worry; different people have different reactions. Some of the differences are a result of your personality, some are due to the actual situation, and some depend on how you have been handling the situation over the years. In a nutshell, if you feel emotional, then that is fine; if you don't feel emotional, that is also fine.

Make sure that you have at least an hour of free time; you do not want to rush the assessment. Take your time. Remember this is an investment in your future. If it has been some time since you read the SHARE chapter (Chapter 7), we suggest that you do that again now to refamiliarize yourself with the principles and rationale. This should help provide guidance about what you are trying to achieve.

Take each topic in turn and complete your assessment on that topic before moving to the next one. Start by writing the word "SHARE" at the top of the page. Then underneath write "Safety".

Safety

Now take a few moments to think about your life. Think about his drinking behaviour.

Does it make you feel unsafe in any way?

For example, he might be violent or aggressive when he has been drinking. Or he might do risky things when intoxicated – driving, cooking, or smoking.

Do you feel that his drinking puts other members of the family – for example, children – at risk of harm?

Spend some time thinking about the situation, about how drinking affects your safety or the safety of others.

Note down anything that occurs to you. Don't try to edit what you write; leave that till later. When you have written everything that concerns you, move to the next heading.

Health

Now take a few moments to think about your life. Think about his drinking behaviour.

Does it affect your health in any way?

Has your physical, psychological, or emotional health suffered? For example, are you gaining/losing weight or suffering from stress, anxiety, or depression?

Does his drinking have an adverse affect on the health of other members of the family – for example, children?

Spend some time thinking about the situation, about how drinking affects your health or the health of your family.

As before, note down anything that occurs to you. Don't try to edit what you write; leave that till later. When you have written everything that concerns you, move to the next heading.

Ambition

Now take a few moments to think about your life. Think about his drinking behaviour.

Does it affect or has it affected your ambitions and aspirations? Do you feel that you could have been wealthier or living in a better house, for example, and that the failure to realize these dreams or ambitions is alcohol-related? Has your life turned out the way you hoped or expected?

Spend some time thinking about the situation, about how drinking affects your ambitions/aspirations and those of other members of your family.

Note down anything that occurs to you. Don't try to edit what you write; leave that till later. When you have written everything that concerns you, move to the next heading.

Relationships

Now take a few moments to think about your life. Think about his drinking behaviour.

Does it affect or has it affected your relationships within or outside the home?

Has it affected your relationship with your partner, with your family, or with your friends? For example, do you feel isolated because of his drinking?

Does it affect or has it affected the relationships of other members of the family – for example, children?

Spend some time thinking about the situation, about how drinking affects your relationships and the relationships of other members of your family.

Note down anything that occurs to you. Don't try to edit what you write; leave that till later. When you have written everything that concerns you, move to the next step.

Environment

Now take a few moments to think about your life. Think about his drinking behaviour.

Does it affect or has it affected your environment – where and how you live?

Has your home suffered because of alcohol? Are there repairs and maintenance tasks that need done? Does he damage the property when he drinks, either deliberately (for example, breaking things in anger) or by accident (for example, burning carpets or furniture by falling asleep while smoking)?

Does his drinking affect or has it affected the environment of other members of the family – for example, children?

Spend some time thinking about the situation, about how drinking affects your environment or the environment of others.

Note down anything that occurs to you. Don't try to edit what you write, leave that till later.

When you are satisfied that you have compiled a comprehensive list of the ways that alcohol is affecting your life, then it is time to prioritize. Look at each category – Safety, Health, Ambition, Relationships, and Environment – in turn. In each of the categories, score each issue on the list on a 1–10 scale where 1 is a small problem (more of an irritation) and 10 a big problem (life- or relationship-threatening). As before, there is no right answer to this. Remember, this is your life and your judgment.

When you have scored each of the items in each of the categories, select the six problems (in any category) with the highest scores. If you have a highlighter pen, use it to highlight these six problems and make them stand out. These are the problems that most concern you. If there is a tie between two or more issues and you cannot decide which is more important, always give preference to the issue that most affects your safety.

At a later stage, you are going to tackle these problems with your drinker. We strongly suggest that this is done in a systematic manner, in manageable chunks. To attempt to tackle all of the problems at once is a step too far. It would overwhelm both you and the drinker, and the process would get swallowed up in too much detail about too many things.

We will discuss in detail how you should go about tackling these issues. However, for the moment you have made a great start on the journey to changing your life and you should congratulate yourself. Now put the assessment aside and leave it for a day or two, a week even. You need to give yourself a chance to absorb what the assessment says and to allow your emotions to settle. There are other assessments that need to be completed before you discuss these issues with your drinker.

Assessing the harm
Part 2

After a week has passed, find a quiet spot and take your notebook. Again, you will again need about an hour during which you will be undisturbed.

In this assessment, you will use the LOVE concept.

Although this is a very different type of assessment, it may be every bit as emotional as SHARE, or even more so. The emotions roused in this assessment may not be exactly the same; there may be more sadness than anger involved. As before, we suggest that you do not try to stifle these feelings. Instead, write down whatever you feel. In a later step, you are going to discuss this assessment with your drinker, so it may be worth noting what you feel and including it in that discussion.

There are three steps to this assessment and they are all very important. Carry out each one in sequence and don't move on till you feel that you have completed that step. If you need to take more time, or you need to take more than one session to finish the assessment, then do that. This is a very important assessment, so do not rush it for the sake of completing the task.

Step 1

You are now going to change your role in this relationship. Through his lies, untrustworthy behaviour, and irresponsibility, and your caretaking and policing, you have adopted roles that are more like parent and errant child rather than the role of partners. You have been the one who has had to be responsible (the parent), who looks after him when he is drunk or recovering. That is about to change. You will prepare to let your "child" look after his own welfare and cut yourself free of the responsibility of looking after him.

Write on the top of the page "Things to let go." Now think of all the things that you do to cover for him, protect him, or clean up after him when he is drinking. It may be waiting around for him to show up for appointments or meals; it may be cooking once he does show up or waiting up to make sure that he makes it to bed. You may make excuses for him to his or your friends. You know what it is that you do.

Now make a list of all these things. You do not need to write them all down in detail (unless, of course, you want to). You are trying to get an idea of where you look after your drinker and in what ways.

Think of all the times you have checked up on his drinking. For example, you may have searched for alcohol hidden around the house or marked the level of bottles (yes, others have done this as well!).

Make a list of these occasions. Now look at each one and decide what you are going to do the next time this happens.

For example, you have cooked and held dinner because he said that he would be home at 7 p.m. What do you do when he does not appear? Do you keep it warm in the event that he will want to eat it when he arrives, or do you put it in the bin and let him make his own? If you need a hint, then it is definitely not the first option!

It is quite possible that everything inside you is screaming "I can't do that, it wouldn't be right!" That is understandable. If you have waited for him and cooked for him for years, it is difficult to stop. However, remember that there is no incentive for him to change if his actions have no consequences. You can just imagine him in the bar thinking "Well, if I'm late, I'll still have my meal made for me. I might get some aggro but I'll still eat. So I'll just have another drink." If, on the other hand, you have changed the pattern, his dialogue becomes "If I stay for another one, my meal is in the bin..."[1] So, yes, it is difficult to make these changes, but it is important for both of you that you do.

Do this for each item on the list and try to imagine yourself letting these things go. They are no longer your responsibility. Just let them go. These things are now his responsibility. If he chooses to drink, then let it be him, and not you, who pays the price. Remember that by letting go you may be helping him, so let them go!

Step 2

Whereas the previous step was about letting go and stopping doing things for him when he is drinking, this step is about doing things together. It is about trying to redress the balance and starting to act more like partners. Partners do things together, plan things together, and spend time together. So you are going to make that kind of behaviour more likely to happen. It will require you to take the initiative and you may still feel that you are operating in the capacity of a parent. We would hope, however, that role should change over time.

Either on a new piece of paper or a new page, write "Optimize our time together." Now think about things that you once liked to do together that did not involve alcohol. Make a list of these things. At this stage don't worry what they are, or how unlikely you are to repeat them; just write them down.

When you are finished, go through the list and cross off anything that might be impossible for you now or that you might not want to repeat. For example, some people may

---

[1] A note of caution. If he becomes aggressive when drunk, we suggest turning the oven off rather than putting the food in the bin. It is less inflammatory.

have loved camping when they were young but loathe the idea now they are older.

Once you have eliminated the less attractive or unrealistic ones, you should be left with a list of possibilities. Is there anything on the list that you would like to do and that you think that he would like to do as well? Try to find a few possibilities – things that could be organized without a great effort, time, or expense.

Write down your shortlist with a few short-term ideas, such as a trip to the cinema, and a few longer-term options, such as a holiday.

Step 3

This step is an attempt to reduce the negative feelings that you probably feel toward your drinker and to reawaken the positive feelings. The anger, the resentment, the lack of trust and respect will colour your view of your drinker and make it difficult to create a positive environment for change. They may make it difficult for you to let go and let him experience the negative consequences. All this emotion may be tinged with guilt, as it feels as if you are acting in an unsupportive way toward him. Ironically, you may feel that Step 2 is also difficult because, although you do not want to be unsupportive, you also don't want to plan nice outings with him. In fact, sometimes you would rather he just wasn't there and you didn't have to think about him.

In the circumstances, these kind of mixed feelings are very common. It is not unusual to hear partners of problem drinkers say "I wish he was dead", and then feel pangs of embarrassment and guilt at having said it. We will stress again: these kind of strong feelings are common, so if you are feeling them, you are not alone.

However, they also need to be handled and this step is part of that process.

Think about what it was that attracted you to him, and vice versa. What were the qualities that you love/loved? Make a list of these qualities. Try not to edit them by saying that he has changed now, particularly if that change is due to the alcohol.

When you have finished the list, spend some time familiarizing yourself with his good qualities. Try to rekindle the feelings of love and affection that you had. (If you are someone who has a faith, this would be a good time to thank God for the good qualities in your partner, even if they are a bit submerged at the moment.)

Congratulations. You have now completed your assessment. Give yourself some time to reflect on what you have discovered. The detail of that answer is only something that you can know. We can venture, however, that you have discovered three things. The first is that alcohol has affected your life more widely than you had realized. The second is that there are many things that you are doing that prevent the drinker from experiencing the negative consequences of alcohol. The third is that there are things that you miss doing and would dearly like to rekindle in your relationship.

In the next two chapters you will use this assessment to create a plan of action, so make a summary of the main points, which you can then use to plan and also use when you meet with your drinker. You will then arrange a meeting with him at which you will start the process of promoting change both in your life and in the life of your drinker.

CHAPTER 9

HOPE in action: Choose your option

In Chapter 8 you carried out a comprehensive assessment of your situation in respect to your partner's drinking. You looked at the damage that it is doing in the various spheres of your life – Safety, Health, Ambitions, Relationships, and Environment. You then looked at the ways that you protected your drinker from the consequences of alcohol. After this, you started to look at things that you and your drinker both enjoyed in the past and that you would like to do again. Finally, you re-examined what were the good qualities and characteristics of your drinker that had attracted you to him and made you fall in love with him.

In this chapter you bring this all together and do your preparation to meet with and talk to your drinker.

You are probably thinking "I'm fed up of talking to him; it never works. I tell him what I think and he doesn't take a blind bit of notice. I've told him repeatedly that things need to change but nothing ever happens, or sometimes there is change but it never lasts."

We are sure that all of the above is perfectly true and you have tried many times. However, it is unlikely that you have tried this method of having a discussion with him. The *Bottled Up* approach is designed to avoid arguments in which the main points that you are trying to make get lost. In arguments, people get caught up in making their own points and trying to get heard. They seldom bother about the points that the other person is trying to make. In other words, they don't listen. This is why arguments seldom solve anything. They are not about reason, logic, or compromise. So if you want to promote change, avoid arguments. Of course, that is easier said than done.

Arguments are more likely to occur when there are strong emotions involved. Some subjects – and drinking is one of them – attract strong emotion, anger, and resentment. So talking about these subjects is often very difficult. The drinker can feel that he is being attacked and accused, which sometimes he is – and, indeed, sometimes he may deserve to be accused. When someone feels that they are under attack, however, they become extremely defensive, and there are few people who are as adept at the art of defensiveness as the problem drinker. He shows this quality particularly well when he feels that he is being criticized unjustly. Indeed, that is when he demonstrates a level of self-righteousness that can be breathtaking!

If you want a hearing and genuinely want to discuss an issue, then how you approach the drinker is crucial. If you approach him in anger, then his attack senses will be alerted and his defensive barriers will be in place before you can make your point. It is much better to approach the drinker in a calm and detached manner and say what you need to say without anger or emotion. If you can do that, you should get a hearing and you should make a start in resolving some issues.

So, what are the options?

In *Bottled Up*, as you know by now, there are two main tools – SHARE and LOVE. It is our hope that you use each of these tools at some time. Although both tools are used to help make your life better, these tools have different goals and different emphasis.

The SHARE tool is primarily concerned with reducing the harmful consequences of drinking. It is not focused on reducing the amount consumed or even the frequency of consumption. Instead, it focuses on changing your drinker's intoxicated behaviour so that you and your family are not harmed, disrupted, or inconvenienced every time your drinker decides to drink.

The LOVE tool is mainly concerned with changing his drinking by getting him to reduce, stop altogether, or even seek help. This is achieved by you letting go of doing things that protect him from experiencing the negative consequences of drinking. You will also come closer to him by arranging activities that you both enjoy and that allow you to spend some quality time together.

SHARE and LOVE are complementary. Both are about giving choice to the drinker and inviting him to behave in a mature and responsible way. They both give the drinker the opportunity to continue drinking. In SHARE, however, you are requesting that the drinking is carried out in a way that does not harm you or your family. We will give some examples of how this can be done. In LOVE, you are giving the drinker a choice: drink or spend time with you.

SHARE or LOVE – which one should I use?

We suggest that you concentrate on SHARE if:

- your drinker is violent, aggressive, or abusive (read the section on Safety in Chapter 7)

- your drinker has been drinking heavily for years

- you have tried on numerous occasions in the past to change the situation with little success

- your drinker disrupts the home when he drinks (define this any way you like)

- there are safety issues when he drinks

- there are a lot of negative consequences, for you and your family, to his drinking.

If any or all of the above statements describe your drinker, then the first priority is SHARE. If, on the other hand, his heavy drinking is a fairly recent behaviour and it does not have a long list of accompanying negative consequences, then you should concentrate more on LOVE.

Even if you feel that SHARE is the most appropriate tool to use at this stage, you should still be using some of your LOVE assessment. There are steps that are common to both approaches. It is the final part of the meeting and the goals that are different. We will give you detailed directions about how to prepare for your meeting(s) and, in the next chapter, how to conduct them.

You need to put aside time to prepare for this meeting. If you were asked to give a speech, you would prepare beforehand and you would probably even rehearse the speech. This could be one of the most important speeches of your life. It could significantly change your life, so put the work in and prepare!

The instructions for the LOVE option can be found below. The instructions for the SHARE option can be found after LOVE.

Preparation for the LOVE option

It is very important that you prepare thoroughly for this meeting as it is likely to be very different from the normal meetings you have with your drinker. Also, if you carry out the steps suggested, it should avoid arguments and fights. Finally, it could be the beginning of change and a new relationship.

Regardless of whether you are going to carry out a LOVE or a SHARE meeting, follow these steps in your preparation. Don't be tempted to skip or stint on this preparation. The better prepared you are, the more confident you will feel and the less chance that you will be drawn into an argument. When you get drawn into an argument, all the good points that you were trying to make get lost and you end up feeling even more frustrated than you were before the meeting. You then say to yourself "That is another method that doesn't work; it's hopeless. I'm hopeless."

Value the drinker

Start by going over your notes for the LOVE exercise. Read back over Step 3. Pick out the most important reasons why you love him. Try to think of times when he showed that particular quality, times when you laughed together, times when you were proud of him, times when you were happy. Write down these qualities and the examples on a new page. You are going to open the meeting with these statements and examples, telling him that you love him and telling him some of the reasons why.

This is a very important step in the meeting. Opening with positive, loving statements should put the meeting on a positive footing from the beginning. It should also reduce the defensiveness in your drinker, which has probably been the source of so many of your arguments. It may be that every time you talked about drinking in the past, he felt that he was being attacked, regardless of whether or not that was your intention. This time, you are approaching it in a very different way. That fact alone should get his attention. There is another reason for opening with these positive statements. For some of you, it may have been a considerable time since you last said positive things to each other. So view it as part of the healing process.

You may be thinking to yourself that this is a problem because you don't really feel that way toward him any more. You did feel that way once, but the years of neglect, abuse, and drinking have now taken their toll. Now you feel angry and bitter at the way he has treated you. That is OK. It is understandable to feel like that. You can still use those statements – just modify them slightly. Instead of saying this is how you feel now, you can say this is how you used to feel and would like to feel again if you could just work toward recapturing that closeness. Obviously, this depends on whether you do actually want to recapture the feelings. (Lou has commented that sometimes when she felt particularly negative, she honoured her husband as the father of her children, whom he loved. That in itself was a positive. You also may have to look hard for the positives sometimes.)

When you have written down your opening – and you may want to write it word for word – it is time to move on to the next step.

Optimize your time with the drinker

In this step you will be putting the responsibility for drinking or not drinking squarely on the shoulders of the drinker. What the optimizing step does is ensure that the choice the drinker makes is highly visible. You are going to offer him an opportunity to spend quality time with you doing things that you both like doing. It makes it very difficult for him to decline without giving you a good reason. This could make him a bit uncomfortable, but remember it is not your job to make things easy and comfortable for him.

To prepare for this step, read over what you wrote in Step 2 about optimizing your time with your drinker. Pick out a couple of things that you enjoyed doing together and a couple of examples from the past. Make sure that it is actually something that he would enjoy but that doesn't need to involve alcohol. Examples might be a romantic dinner at home or in a restaurant, or a long walk on a nearby beach or in the countryside. Write down one or two of these options and put a timescale to them – for example, in the next week.

When you organize these sessions, always have a fallback plan. Let's say you plan a romantic dinner for two at home. You ask him to come home by 7 p.m. to eat at 7.30 p.m. You tell him that you really want to have a lovely evening together, just the two of you. The only thing that you ask is that he does not drink before he comes home or during the evening. If he agrees, then you prepare a meal, and if he arrives on time and sober, then have a lovely evening.

If, instead, he does not arrive on time or comes home after a drinking session (it is up to you how much drinking you think is acceptable), then eat your meal and go out. You may give his to the dog if you wish (remembering the warning we gave before). In advance of the evening, make sure that you arrange with a close friend that you may need to call round for the evening. Tell the friend exactly what you have planned and ask them if they could keep some time free.

Arrange another meal for the following week. Again, make arrangements with a friend in case he does not keep to the bargain. However, this week he knows from the previous week's experience that the dog will enjoy his dinner if he does not turn up.

It does not matter what you have planned, but make sure that you have a contingency plan if he drinks or does not show. From now on you do not spend your time waiting around for him. You make alternative plans and make sure he knows that you enjoyed yourself.

Remember this step is all about choice. If he chooses to drink, then you will choose to enjoy yourself in other ways.

Letting the drinker experience the negative consequences

For many people, this is a difficult step. For years they have been taking care of the drinker, ensuring that he did not injure himself or get himself in trouble. Now they are being asked to step back and allow the naturally occurring consequences of drinking to happen. To some, this can appear like betrayal. As we have already discussed, however, change in problem drinkers most often occurs when the negatives of the drinking outweigh the positives. If you are shielding the drinker, then he is not experiencing these negatives and so change is less likely.

Read over your notes on Step 1 about letting the drinker experience negative consequences. Select a couple of examples of where you have protected, provided for, or cleaned up after him. Write these down as well, along with your plans on how you will handle future instances. Be quite specific about what you will and won't do.

One of the ways you may have been protecting the drinker is by hiding your problems and his drinking from your friends and relations. You may have done this by making excuses for him, or you may have refused invitations to gatherings for fear that he would drink too much. So you may have isolated yourself. You should now think about renewing some of these friendships and no longer covering up his drinking. All of us could use friends, especially when we have problems such as living with a problem drinker. So let them into your life again. They probably know much more than you think they do and were just waiting for you to give them permission to help. Make a list of people you will contact.

Now make sure that your notes are organized into a logical format. When you meet with your drinker you want to:

1. Start with positive statements about either how you love him and why or how you loved him and why you would like to again.

2. Make it clear that you would like to spend some time together doing things that you both like and building your relationship, but if he chooses to drink, then you will make a life of your own.

3. Explain that you are no longer going to protect him from the negative consequences of alcohol or hide your or his problems from your friends or relatives.

4. When you have completed this exercise, you should now have your notes ready for a meeting with your drinker. If you want to follow the LOVE option, read the next chapter about getting the best from your meeting.

Preparation for the SHARE option

Just as with the LOVE option, it is important to prepare well for the meeting with the drinker. This section provides the instructions for that meeting. The SHARE option is less concerned about getting the drinker to cut down or stop drinking. It is more concerned with reducing the harmful consequences of drinking for you and your family.

The SHARE option starts the same way as the LOVE option: by valuing the drinker. For full instructions on this step and the rationale, read "Value the drinker" in the LOVE option above.

In the SHARE option, we don't try to organize time together. We hope that this is something that you will return to at a later date. For the moment, it would only distract from the principal goal of SHARE which is to reduce the negative consequences of drinking for yourself and your family. Instead, we proceed to letting the drinker experience the negative consequences of his drinking. Refer to "Let the drinker experience the negative consequences" in the LOVE option above.

SHARE

In Chapter 8 you carried out the SHARE assessment and selected the six problems with the highest scores. These are the biggest problems for you. At this stage it might be better to reduce this list three; six may be too many to tackle at this first meeting.

Look at these problems individually. Is there a way that you could reduce the impact of that behaviour? (Remember, we are not talking about stopping drinking at this stage.) Let us look at a couple of examples.

Let's say that your drinker goes to a bar and has a few drinks, then comes home and lounges in front of the TV to continue his drinking. This can cause a problem for you sitting with someone who is getting drunker, and it could also cause a problem for any children in the house. You could negotiate with your drinker, saying that you are not very happy with him coming in after drinking in the bar and drinking more on the sofa. You are willing to compromise, however. When he has been drinking, you won't bother him if he wants to continue drinking, but his compromise is that he takes himself to another room away from where the family is.

Another example could be that your drinker, like many drinkers, gets hungry when he drinks. The result is that he cooks, using the frying pan or deep-fat fryer. You fear that he might start a fire and burn himself or damage the house. There can be many compromises here. One might be that he prepares something earlier and microwaves it. You could even provide some sandwiches (it is the lesser of two evils). You could leave microwaveable meals for him. Remember, this is about harm reduction and safety. We discuss this and other safety issues in Chapter 11.

Look at the problems you have highlighted and try to think of some possible solutions. Once you have finished, you are ready to meet with your drinker. However, we suggest that you read and digest the next chapter before arranging a meeting.

CHAPTER 10

HOPE in action: Promoting change and evaluation

In the Chapters 8 and 9 you carried out a thorough assessment using the tools SHARE and LOVE. You then prepared notes for a meeting with your drinker. These notes were based on your chosen option for the meeting. You may have chosen SHARE, where the goal is about reducing the harmful consequences of drinking, or LOVE, where the goal is to get him to change his drinking and improve your relationship.

In this chapter we will discuss the actual meeting and how to ensure maximum success. It is very important to realize that it is unlikely that one meeting (whether SHARE or LOVE) is going to change everything. It is better to view the meeting as the beginning of a process rather than as an end in itself. Change can take time to happen and it can take even longer to become stable. So exercise your patience and positivity.

Before

Arrange the meeting at a time and place where you will have no distractions. Ideally, your drinker will not have been drinking, but if he drinks all the time, then make it a time when he has had relatively little alcohol. If he is drunk, do not have the meeting; it is a waste of your time. If you have children, try to pick a time when they will not be around. It would be worth getting a friend or relative to take them out for a couple of hours so that you are not interrupted.

Make sure you feel calm and composed; this is possibly the most important predictor of how well the meeting will go. He is probably expecting a meeting that is similar to your previous discussions – lots of shouting, accusations, and tears. If you do not think that you can contain your anger, do not have the meeting; wait till you can approach it in a calm manner. Again, this is important. You are trying to establish a new style of communication, one where you can discuss drinking in a calm and rational manner. So it is important that you are assertive (say your piece calmly but firmly) rather than aggressive or submissive.

One way to help you to stay calm is to write down exactly what you want to say and keep to the script. Even read it if it helps. Having a script should help you not to get sidetracked into other issues. Also, if your partner mishears or misquotes you, you have something written down that you can refer him to.

Below are instructions for the two different types of meetings, SHARE and LOVE. Try to follow them as closely as possible.

SHARE

Tell your drinker that you want to discuss your relationship and how you believe it could be improved. Say that you have some suggestions, but there are some things that you want to say first. Your drinker may be very defensive at this point, especially if you have a history of arguments and fights about drinking. He may be expecting another lecture, nagging, or fight. Your job at this stage is to reduce his defensiveness and the best way to do that is through saying positive things.

Start by saying that you are not going to ask him to stop drinking, or even cut down his drinking. Tell him that if he wants to continue to drink, that is his choice and this meeting is not designed to persuade him otherwise.

Read the positive things that you have noted. These are some of the reasons why you love(d) him. Tell him what it was about him that attracted you. Give the examples. Tell him that you really want that person back, that you know he is still there.

Now give him an opportunity to respond. Ask him what he thinks about what you have said. If he responds in a positive fashion, then that is great. However, if he doesn't respond in the way you hoped, do not get drawn into an argument. For example, he may say that he is exactly the same as he always was; he may even suggest that you are the one who has changed. Just say that that is an interesting point of view and move on.

Now tell your drinker that, in an ideal world, you would rather that he did not drink any more. As you stated at the beginning, however, you do realize that this is completely his choice. One of the conditions of him exercising his choice to drink is that you are now going to start exercising your choice also. You are going to exercise your choice about how you live your life. Therefore, if he does decide to continue drinking, from now on you will not be protecting him, cleaning up after him, or providing for him when he drinks. You can then read out what you have written about letting go. Again, do not get drawn into an argument. Just say what you need to say and move to the next topic.

This is where you introduce your assessment from SHARE. Begin with the first issue which should be the one that is most important to you, the one that you scored highest in SHARE.

Tell him about the issue and why it is important to you. Do not be aggressive or confrontational when you discuss it. Instead, be calm and clear. You have got him to the meeting; don't spoil it now by turning it into an argument.

Say what you feel about the issue. For example, if he smokes in bed when drinking, say "I get really frightened when you are drinking in case you come to bed and smoke. I just can't sleep while you are awake. I just lie there, scared that you are going to fall asleep and set fire to the bed and the house."

Or, if your issue is his heavy drinking when you are with friends, say "I am beginning to feel that I have almost no social life any more. Alice and David phoned to ask us to dinner but I felt that I had to say no. Every time we go there we have an argument about how much you drink."

Then ask "How can we change (whatever the issue is)?"

Listen respectfully to any suggestions that are put forward. There just may be a few good ideas and workable solutions. If there are no solutions forthcoming, then you should have a couple of your own ready. Tell him what they are. For the first issue, for example, you might get him to promise that he won't smoke in the bedroom any more. For the second issue, you might say that you are going to start accepting invitations, and although you would really prefer him to accompany you and not drink, you accept that this could be a problem for him. You will therefore go on your own in future. He is welcome to join you any time he wants to, provided he does not drink (or cuts down).

When you have finished presenting your issues, you can ask him how he feels about what you have said. If he responds positively, then you may want to discuss it further. If, instead, he responds negatively, don't get drawn into an argument. Just say calmly but firmly that he is welcome to make his choices and that you will be making your choices. Then thank him for listening. You have now said all that you wanted to say and you can walk away.

LOVE

Tell your drinker that you want to discuss your relationship and how you believe it could be improved. Say that you have some suggestions, but there are some things that you want to say first. Your drinker may be very defensive at this point, especially if you have a history of arguments and fights about drinking. They may be expecting another lecture, nagging, or fight. Your job at this stage is to reduce the defensiveness, and the best way to do that is through saying positive things.

Start by saying that you are not going to ask him to stop drinking or even cut down his drinking. Tell him that if he wants to continue to drink, that is his choice and this meeting is not designed to persuade him otherwise.

Read the positive things that you have noted. These are some of the reasons why you love(d) him. Tell him what it was about him that attracted you. Give the examples. Tell him that you really want that person back, that you know he is still there.

Now give him an opportunity to respond. Ask him what he thinks about what you have said. If he responds in a positive fashion, then that is great. However, if he doesn't respond in the way you hoped, do not get drawn into an argument. For example, he may say that he is exactly the same as he always was; he may even suggest that you are the one who has changed. Just say that that is an interesting point of view and move on.

Now read the things you wrote about your previous activities. These are the things that you did together. He might miss them as well. Tell him that you would really like to be closer and that you would love to do some of these things again. Ask him what he thinks about that.

Now tell him you have some plans that will involve spending more time together and this is something that you really want to do. Tell him the plans and see what his reaction is. If it is positive, then tell him that you really want to do these things, but the only thing you ask is that there should be no drinking on these occasions.

Now tell your drinker that, in an ideal world, you would rather that he did not drink any more. As you stated at the beginning, however, you do realize that this is completely his choice. One of the conditions of him exercising his choice to drink is that you are now going to start exercising your choice too. You are going to exercise your choice about how you live your life. Therefore, if he does decide to continue drinking, from now on you will not be protecting him, cleaning up after him, or providing for him when he drinks. You can then read out what you have written about letting go. Again, do not get drawn into an argument. Just say what you need to say and move on.

Finally, read out what you have written in your summary. You can say that you love him because...; you loved being with him especially when he/you...; that you would love to...; however, if he continues to drink, you will/won't... It may be useful to give him a copy of this summary as well.

Try to be calm through this and finish on a positive note, but remind him that the outcome is his choice.

Read the following tips to help you carry this exercise off well.

Tips to avoid derailment

- Phrases such as "I feel..." or "This affects me..." are generally far less emotive than "You are doing this..." or "You are making me (angry, hurt, upset)". The latter sound much more blaming and accusatory, which will trigger defensiveness.

- It is a good idea to write your points down exactly the way you are going to say them. "I feel threatened if you smoke cigarettes when you're drinking" could be quoted back to you as "You accused me of burning the house down" when processed through his negative and defensive framework. "Look, it is written here" is a more useful response than entering into an "I didn't"/"Yes, you did" argument.

- Don't be rushed. Take all the time you need, but keep things paced; otherwise your partner may lose focus.

- When you are talking about standing back from protecting and caretaking behaviour, it might be helpful to explain that not only is it not fair for these things to continue, but that leaving these situations alone should reduce the level of anger that you feel about his drinking. Therefore, it is not only good for you but also good for him and the relationship. This could avoid the sense of implied threat he might read into this part of the meeting.

- If you feel he is becoming too defensive or turning things around on you, try not to stalk off in disgust (however tempting this may be at the time). Thank him for listening to the things he has taken on board and suggest a time for another meeting soon. Don't increase the cycle of failure and disappointment.

- Don't despair if you don't see change immediately. Remember that it has probably taken years to establish the drinking behaviours, so it may take a few meetings before you start to achieve your goals.

Evaluation

After your meeting, let some time pass for everything that was said to be absorbed. Don't expect change immediately, because you could be leaving yourself open to disappointment. However, you should decide how long you are willing to wait to see some signs of change. It is hard to make any meaningful recommendation that is suitable for all types of drinkers and patterns of drinking. For example, your drinker may be a daily drinker, in which case you would hope to see some kind of change in his behaviour within a week. This would be particularly relevant if you had used SHARE and the changes you asked for concerned safety. If, on the other hand, your drinker is a binge drinker with dry periods of up to a couple of weeks, then obviously a week is inappropriate.

Whatever the period you choose, be realistic. You should then look for change in the areas of behaviour that you discussed during the meeting. For example, has he changed his behaviour so that you feel safer? Or, if your meeting was mainly about LOVE, has he turned up for the outings or events that you arranged? Did he turn up sober and stay sober throughout the event?

If the answer to these questions is no, there has been no change at all, don't despair! As we have said before, change takes time. Organize another meeting and repeat your script from the previous meeting. You may need to do this a few times.

If, however, the answer is yes, then that is great! It is time to move to the next meeting. If you are using the SHARE approach, then take the next most serious problems from your list. If you are using the LOVE approach, then look at what has been most successful and, if appropriate, repeat it and add in a new date and time.

You should also evaluate your own behaviour as well. Have you managed to let go successfully? Have you found yourself worrying less, sleeping better, not checking what he is drinking or at least checking less often? Are you going out more often? Are you finding new interests? Have you recruited support? If the answer to all of these questions is yes, then well done indeed. If the answer is no, then add that to your "to do" list for the coming month.

After a couple of months have passed, you may want to redo your assessment. Try to do this without looking at your previous assessment. When you have completed the new assessment, look at the two side by side. Has anything changed? What now needs to be done?

This completes our discussion of the HOPE cycle. For you it is just the beginning. We created this tool as a circle because that is the nature of change. You need to keep chipping away at it by assessing the Harm, choosing the right Option, Promoting change, Evaluating the effect. How many times you need to go round the cycle is impossible to tell. It depends on you and your drinker. We trust, though, that these tools will speed that process.

CHAPTER 11

Breaking the cycle: Some frequently asked questions

In this chapter we will do something a bit different. We will look at a few scenarios – some that may be familiar to you, some that may not. They are questions that we have been commonly asked both on the website and in other spheres of our lives.

It is important to appreciate that we are not trying to provide you with definitive answers that you should use in these situations. Instead, our intention is to provide a few possible solutions that may spark some ideas about ways to handle your own situations. The type of solutions that you use and that are ideal for you will emerge from your interaction with your drinker. Try to think a bit differently. For some situations, particularly when safety is involved, you may need to be pragmatic. That may mean that you need to do things that you don't really agree with. Indeed, you may disagree quite strongly with some of the suggestions that we have put forward. Just remember, it is your life, your situations, and your solutions. Don't worry about other people judging you and saying that you did it wrong. You do not need to conform to someone else's idea of what is or isn't right. If it works for you and you are happy with it, then that is what matters. Lastly, please note that each question stands alone and the order is random; there is no suggestion of priority or importance.

Should I talk to the children about their father's drinking?

This is a question that often arises. It is a difficult question and, like all the answers we give here and elsewhere, there is no blanket answer for everyone. You know your situation and your children better than anyone and you are in the best position to decide. In order to make that decision, however, we have suggested a few things that you may want to think about.

Unless your children are very young, they probably know some of what is going on already – almost certainly a lot more than you think. However, some of what they believe may be distorted, and talking to them openly about what is happening may be a way of giving them the correct information and clearing up some misconceptions.

If you have recently become less patient or more critical than usual, then it may be useful for your children to know that you are under a bit of stress and that they are not the cause of your impatience. Your children may be concerned and even frightened by what is happening. Talking about it may be an opportunity to reassure them.

To take a broader view, if we deal with problems by hiding them and/or pretending they don't exist, then we have to ask ourselves what that teaches our children about dealing with their own problems in later life.

Your children may be one of your best assets for promoting change in the drinker. We do not mean you should use them as a weapon, but instead include them in family days out when working through LOVE. This may be actually very tempting for the drinker.

Finally, if you do decide to tell them, it is best to do it in an even-handed way. Just as we suggest using LOVE to approach your drinker, it may be best to use some of these strategies when talking to the children. For example, talk about how their father loves them and how he is a good man who has problems. You could then suggest how they might be supportive to you and their father. That way they become part of the solution rather than being excluded.

Obviously, none of this is ideal. Bringing children more fully into the picture may reduce both your stress and theirs, and have the advantage of clarifying the exact nature of the tense atmosphere that they have almost certainly been picking up. Nevertheless, it does increase the sense of heartbreak too.

In the early days, Lou would just scoop the children up and take them out of the way. However, she distinctly remembers the time that she felt that telling her children was inevitable. It was then hard to watch them trying the same strategies with their father that she had so often tried in the past – pleading, punishing, and so on – then watching as they realized that their father was not going to modify his behaviour for them either, even though he loved them. Overall, though, it was much less stressful for everyone having the whole family on board.

Whom should I tell about his drinking?

Rather than answer that question directly, we will approach it in a rather different way, by asking another question. Why would you tell anyone? Until now you have probably guarded your secret well. You will have been trying to avoid the shame and guilt that we talked about in Chapter 2. Are we now suggesting that you expose your shame to public scrutiny? You can react to that in a number of different ways.

The first type of reaction, and the most obvious, is to say to yourself "No way, that seems just too scary." Of course, that is a very understandable reaction and nobody could blame you for it. But, as we explained before, it is by not bottling it up any more that you will be set free from that guilt and shame.

A second reaction is to see this as a real opportunity to get even. You have been hiding *his* secrets, picking up guilt that was really *his*. Now you will tell the world what he is like. You won't feel guilty any more. You will make sure that the blame falls squarely on *his* shoulders. Again understandable, but not quite what we had in mind. This is about freedom, not revenge.

The third, and the one that we would suggest, is that you welcome disclosure as an opportunity for healing. So you plan to tell *selected* people. Tell the people you are close to, your best friends or relatives. These are the ones who will give you a hearing and support when you need it. They are the first group that you should be disclosing to, and the sooner the better. A second group may be those people you see on a regular basis. People who, if you don't tell them, could make it difficult for you because you would feel that you needed to avoid them or lie to them, which would bring more guilt and shame. They may be friends you are not so close to, neighbours, or people who work for you or with you. You should decide whom to tell on the principle that you are not going to lie or cover for him any more. Just beware of the spark of spite coming out and avoid telling people who you think could make things more difficult for you – those, for example, who you know are gossips. You want to free yourself from shame, not substitute it for a different kind.

So are you saying that if his drinking is bad, I should just be quiet and say nothing to him?

No, we are not saying that at all, and we sincerely hope that it doesn't sound as if we are saying that you should just accept what is happening. One of the main intentions of *Bottled Up* is to empower you; it is not to make your position even worse than it already is. What we are saying is that trying to change your drinker's behaviour by using the 4 Ps (discussed in Chapter 3) is not likely to be effective. What we want to do is empower you by showing you a new method that is more effective. Using this new *Bottled Up* approach, you will be able to make your feelings and wishes felt in a way that should be more effective in terms of communicating and in bringing about change.

I have read about another method of changing behaviour that consists of getting his family and friends round and confronting him about his behaviour. What about that method?

Research on that method has shown it to be effective in some cases. If you can organize this type of confrontation, then it is difficult for the drinker to ignore what is being said to him. This is particularly true if the confrontation is done in a kind and loving manner. If it is done in an angry or dogmatic manner, it can cause even more problems than it solves.

The problem with this approach is not that it does not work, but rather that most people can't organize it or they do not go through with it. The confrontation may not happen through fear of the possible repercussions, fear of having to disclose to all those people, not wanting to bring others into your private affairs, or any number of other reasons. Sadly, this can leave you feeling even more impotent. If you can organize one of these confrontations and you use the principles of LOVE (start by telling him he is loved, that you would rather do things as a family, for example), then by all means give it a go as it provides another option. However, it can be a bit like putting all your eggs in one basket, hoping for the big change. As we have said before in this book, change is a process, not an event!

He keeps telling me that he is going to get help, stop drinking, make changes, but nothing ever happens.

There can be few things more demoralizing than this. You have waited patiently for something to happen, some change. You begin to reconcile yourself to the problems by not allowing your hopes and expectations to get too high. Then you are told that what you have been wanting all this time is at last about to happen. You start to hope, to believe. You let your guard down. Then – nothing! It hurts; it hurts badly. You are vulnerable, your defences are down, and this disappointment seems unbearable.

For these reasons we suggest that you try to learn to detach. You cannot spend your time hoping that today is the day that he will change, whether he is saying that or not. If you live waiting to see if he will drink, how much he will drink, whether he will go to the doctor, and then reacting accordingly, then that is not much of a life. Learn that he may need to say that he is going to change many, many times before anything actually happens. So try to practise detachment. When he does say "I am going to stop drinking, go for help..." perhaps you could just say "Don't tell me what you are going to do, show me."

He drives drunk and, what is worse still, he takes the children in the car.

Driving while under the influence is dangerous, not just to him but also to other road users. If he takes the children as well, then he is putting their lives at risk. We believe that you have a number of ways of tackling this. Each of the suggestions below is a progressively stronger measure if the previous one does not work.

First, we suggest that you use LOVE and SHARE and put your fears to him. You could ask him not to drive when he is drunk, or, better still, you could ask him to give you the car keys if he is going to be drinking. If necessary, you may need to agree to drive him if he needs/wants to go somewhere. Again, this is not ideal but it is about pragmatism and safety.

The next option is to discuss with the children (depending on their ages) that you do not want them to get into the car with their father. Tell them that they must ask you first before driving with him. Again, your priority is to keep the children safe.

Sometimes we need to make some very difficult decisions and this last one is in that category. If you have tried everything and he still drinks and drives *and* drives with the children, then your last option may be to phone the police. He is going to be really mad if the police stop him and arrest him for being over the limit. However, you need to weigh his anger against how you would feel if your children were injured or, worse, killed in an accident. You could discuss this scenario as part of your SHARE meeting with him and tell him clearly that you would rather that it did not come to it, but you will phone the police if he takes the children in the car when he has been drinking. That way he has been warned and the threat may be deterrent enough if he believes that you are serious.

We are broke all the time because he drinks all the money.

Drinking heavily takes a lot of money. Unfortunately, as drinkers become more dependent on alcohol, their conscience about spending money that is meant for the home, rent, or food tends to be dulled. If there is money easily available by using a cheque book or credit card, then they will spend it.

You could address this issue through SHARE and LOVE. Organize a meeting with your drinker and discuss the issue with him. Remember to be calm and detached but firm. Tell him that you are concerned about your family finances and that you would like him to be concerned as well. If he says that he *is* concerned, then you have a number of options that you can put to him.

The weakest agreement, but better than nothing, is that he will agree to spend less or, better still, an agreed limit per week or month. Nevertheless, you have every right to be sceptical of such promises.

You want to control the credit/debit cards, so ask him to give his cards to you. A recent innovation is the prepaid credit card. You use it like a credit card but it has to be paid prior to use. Intended to help people prone to getting into debt, it can be obtained free from some phone and other companies. This could be a solution for a drinker.

If possible, get him to agree to put the bank account into your name. If he won't agree to that, then try to get him to agree to a sum of money being transferred at the beginning of every month into a bank account to which he has no access.

If he agrees to any of these options, then get it done immediately or as soon as possible.

I have stopped going to social functions because he embarrasses himself and me.

It is very tempting, and understandable, to stay away from social functions to avoid embarrassment, but that only increases your sense of isolation and frustration. An alternative way to handle this is by using the LOVE concept. As we saw in Chapter 6, L stands for Letting the drinker take responsibility for his own drinking. If he gets drunk and his behaviour is embarrassing, then the embarrassment is *his*, not yours! You need not and should not take the responsibility for his behaviour – this is his problem. Do not defend him, or try to cover for him, and definitely do not take responsibility for him. Do not try to hide the fact that he drinks too much, too often. Tell your friends about the problems. You are not being disloyal to him; you are being true to you. If he wants that kind of loyalty, he shouldn't drink!

Another way of handling it is to tell him beforehand that you will go to the event and he is very welcome to come and drink as little or as much as he likes. You would prefer that he did not drink at the function (or did not drink to excess). If he does choose to drink to excess, then you will leave him and go home. The choice is now his. If he does drink too much, then leave him to it and either try to enjoy yourself or go home. After you have done this a couple of times he should get the message.

This isn't working! I've tried but we are not going anywhere.

There could be a couple of things happening here, depending on how long you have been trying the *Bottled Up* approach. If you've been doing this for only a couple of weeks, then perhaps this situation needs patience. Change takes time. It has taken a long time to establish the patterns of behaviour that you and your drinker carry out, and it will take some time for the patterns to be broken and for new behaviour patterns to be established. First of all, check that you have applied LOVE and SHARE in the way suggested, but also remember that it is unlikely that LOVE and SHARE will work wonders with only one meeting. You are almost certainly going to need a few meetings (how many depends on you, your drinker, and your history). If you have applied LOVE and SHARE as suggested, then ask yourself if there is really no change at all. Is he more amenable? Can you discuss things without argument? Has there been any reduction in his drinking or change in his behaviour? If the answer to any of these questions is yes but not much, then maybe you just need to give it a bit more time.

If the answer is no – there has been no change despite your best efforts – then it may be time to look at other options. We sincerely hope that using LOVE and SHARE will rekindle relationships and make them stronger. However, we do not believe that you need to hang on in there at all costs. You do not need yet another guilt trip. So what are your options?

Your options will vary according to your circumstances, family, and finances. The next section discusses the options for partners. Advice for other family members is given in the section following.

Options for partners

One possible option is to remove yourself from the home for a period of time. You can discuss the position with your drinker and tell him that you can't continue to live this way. You need some peace of mind and a break from the worry and uncertainty. If it is the case that you would like to repair the relationship, then tell him so and say that you would like to come back, but only if he does something about his drinking. You would like to be with the man you love, but you have chosen not to be with the drinker he has become. It is now up to him whether he chooses to continue to drink or to be with you.

This may be a difficult option if you have children and,

ideally, you should negotiate that he is the one who leaves. You should also try to get the house put in your name so that you can have him removed if he comes back drunk. If you get to this stage, he may offer promises of change. You would then need to think very hard about whether you would be willing to accept these promises. After all, it is your experience of his inability or unwillingness to change that has brought you to this option. Whichever of the above you choose, we strongly advise that you first consult a solicitor if at all possible. Some actions will have repercussions if you end up separating from or divorcing your partner.

The last option in this section is one that we hope you will not need to pursue: that is, separation or divorce. This is different from the previous option where your intention is to be reunited in the future when he sorts himself out. In this option there is no such intention. If this is the option that you need to take, then we hope that you have carried out HOPE, LOVE, and SHARE. If you have tried, then you will be able to look back, probably with sadness, but also in the knowledge that you tried your best to make things right. It is amazing how much guilt remains after separation or divorce, even if the breakdown of the relationship is primarily triggered by drink-related problems. Any work that you put into repairing your relationship now, even if it doesn't eventually work out, will help at a later date to reassure you and your family: "I did the best I could."

What advice would you give to other family members?

We feel that much of what we present in this book is appropriate for other members of the family as well as partners. Some of the programme of HOPE, LOVE, and SHARE may need to be adapted to fit individual circumstances, but the principles are the same – for example, let him experience the negative consequences, or optimize your time with the drinker by offering alternatives.

Parents of adult children with drinking problems

If he is married, encourage his partner to apply SHARE and LOVE and offer whatever support needed to apply these most effectively. Try not to over-defend your drinking "child" or over-collude with the partner. Try to stay detached and fair, supportive and available (within reason – don't exhaust yourself).

Parents with drinking teenagers

Again apply LOVE and SHARE. Be careful not to overprotect or rescue, as this means that the drinker will be less likely to face the consequences of his own behaviour. If you set boundaries that are consistently broken, it may be appropriate to ask the drinker to leave the family home. This does not need to mean putting him out on the streets, but it may mean helping him find the deposit for a bedsit or a flat. This will be very painful and difficult to contemplate, but in the final analysis it may be better than being dragged into a state of physical or mental exhaustion. Counselling or support of other close family members could be helpful here.

Brothers/sisters

There may be less of a collateral relationship as your day-to-day lives may be less involved with a sibling. You could encourage him to look at 24/7 Help Yourself (www.247helpyourself.com) or elsewhere for help. Try not to overprotect or collude with your sibling. Try not to rescue and try to provide alternatives to drinking. Support your parents as much as possible.

Teens

If the drinker is a parent, then try to support your non-drinking parent. We strongly suggest that you talk to a school counsellor or your doctor, so that you are not going through this alone. You could join Alateen for support and help.

CHAPTER 12

Stepping out of the shadow

This chapter should be seen as a companion chapter to LOVE (Chapter 6). It is especially relevant to the "Let go" part of LOVE but it also fits with "Optimize your time with the drinker." But mostly this chapter is aimed at encouraging you to look after *you*, build a support network, boost your self-esteem, and make a life for yourself that is independent of the drinker. On the surface, that appears to be completely at odds with optimizing your time with the drinker but, as we will explain later in the chapter, there is no contradiction.

One of the problems of living with a problem drinker is that it can completely take over your life and leave little or no time for yourself. It is a full-time occupation worrying if he will drink, if he does drink, whether he will get drunk, and if he does get drunk, whether he will embarrass himself and you. Will he injure himself, damage something? What time will he come home? What state will he be in? Will he make it home? Is he really an alcoholic? Is it just me? Am I a nag? How can I get him to change? The list could go on and on.

You may also feel increasingly isolated as your world seems to shrink. Where are all the friends and relations who once called round or invited you to parties? Have you cut yourself off as the stigma and shame of his drinking has grown? If you are a parent, do you feel trapped in the house with the kids because you can't trust him not to drink when he is in charge?

If you recognize this state of anxiety and isolation, you are not alone. Many people who live with problem drinkers find themselves in a very similar position.

Co-dependency

If you become familiar with the different aspects of problem drinking, sooner or later you will come across the term "co-dependency". There has been a lot of confusion around this term, so please bear with us as we try to unpack it a bit more. Some people view the behaviours described at the beginning of this chapter (such as worrying and isolating yourself) as symptoms of co-dependency. There are various views about what co-dependency is, including the views of some who question whether it is even a real condition. At one extreme it is believed to be a "disease" that is in place long before the relationship with the drinker. Co-dependent people have an inability to form healthy relationships, usually as a result of growing up in a dysfunctional family. In this view, they seek a relationship with a drinker or some other unreliable person because they need to "caretake" and control someone. The drinker fulfils that need and provides a purpose and role for the co-dependant.

Others also see it is a "disease" but one that is caused

by living with a person who has an addiction. According to this view, other people get slowly drawn into his world and his addiction, and the need for control in their lives leads to psychological and emotional problems.

A less pathological view is that living with a person with an addiction brings a whole set of difficulties, and it is not surprising that someone's behaviour would change. However, persistence with these behaviours and attempts to change him lead to frustration, depression, learned helplessness, anxiety, and so on.

In *Bottled Up* we believe that for most people this last view is the most relevant. That is, we believe that much of the behaviour known as co-dependency is a "normal" response to an extremely difficult situation.

In no way do we deny that, for some, co-dependency may well be a condition that exists prior to the partnership with the drinker. If you find yourself unable to sustain intimate relationships, it may be advisable to seek further help. For the majority of you, however, a change of behaviour should be sufficient to reduce the worst of the symptoms of co-dependency. Many of these symptoms arise from repeated ineffectual attempts to control and contain the addictive behaviour, and in this book we are trying to show you different, more productive ways to react and behave.

One of the main characteristics of co-dependent behaviour is that it tends to perpetuate the addiction. Obviously, this is not the intention of the behaviour but it does tend to be the result. As we discussed in Chapter 3, repeated unsuccessful attempts at controlling the drinker's consumption have been observed to lead to particular patterns of behaviour in the partner. These are:

- *Controlling behaviour* – It is natural for you to want control of your environment and your life. However, trying to control a drinker's behaviour tends to lead to arguments because he feels that he is being demeaned and distrusted, and this makes him want to rebel against any controls.

- *Perfectionism* – This means you need to get it right all the time, and so does everyone else. The fact that this is not happening brings out continually more desperate attempts at control.

- *Avoidance of feelings* – For example, you will find yourself continually saying "I'm all right, I'm fine." If we don't acknowledge feelings, we feel that maybe they will go away.

- *Intimacy problems* – You start to avoid sexual or intimate behaviours and feelings.

- *Hyper-vigilance* – The drinker's behaviour is a constant source of worry. Contingency plans are continually being made in the event of his drinking. Little attention is left for yourself.

- *Physical and/or psychological illness related to stress* – Eventually, all of the above behaviours will take their toll, physically and emotionally. Sleep patterns and diet are often the first to go, so there is weight loss or gain. Anxiety, sometimes accompanied by depression, is also common.

Although there does appear to be a "co-dependency syndrome", we believe that, for most partners of problem drinkers, this label is unnecessary and inappropriate. Most of you have troubles aplenty without adding a psychological diagnosis to them. So rather than concentrate on "the condition", we intend to spend the remainder of the chapter discussing possible ways of reversing or addressing it. If you would like to find out more about co-dependency or some of the other topics discussed here, you will find a list of resources at the end of the book.

He is no longer your responsibility

As we discussed at the opening of this chapter, living with a problem drinker can be a full-time occupation that can leave you feeling isolated. It is less like a partnership and more akin to having the guardianship of an errant child. If you are going to have a life of your own, the first thing you need to do is let go of your "naughty child".

In the chapters about LOVE, you were asked to look at what you did for your drinker, where you covered for him, protected him, and cleared up after him. We discussed how this protected him from the negative consequences of drinking, which could be delaying him changing his behaviour. You were then asked to tell him that you would not be doing this in future. It was now time for him to clear up after himself and accept whatever consequences his drinking brought. The time has now arrived for you to stand back and leave him to it, but there is more to it than that.

Have you ever been at a party or a night out and your drinker has consumed much more than he should have? Of course you have, and you have probably felt guilty and embarrassed by his conduct. You may even have apologized to everyone at the party. Deep inside you are angry, but mostly you feel shame, deep and crushing shame. The next time you go to a function, you have *that* conversation as you leave. "Please watch what you drink tonight, will you?" And somehow when he says "Of course I will; I'll be fine", this does not reassure at all. Your trepidation is not reduced one little bit. In fact, you spend the whole evening watching his every move, counting his drinks, and waiting for the worst to happen. Sometimes it will and sometimes it won't, but always you will be waiting for it.

This is another area where you should let go. The guilt and the shame are not yours: they are, or at least should be, his. Instead of having *that* conversation, try saying "It is completely up to you what you do this evening. If you drink too much, I will not be apologizing for you. You are a big boy now, so make your own choices." You can then detach from what he is doing. If someone points out that he is drinking too much, just tell them that it is his choice.

You are almost certainly thinking "I wish I could do that, but it is easier said than done." We completely agree! This is a huge ask. However, remember that you dearly want him to change his behaviour, so this may give you some insight into the difficulty that he faces as well. It would be exceptional if you were to manage this the first time you try, so don't worry if you get it wrong. Continue to work at it, letting it go more and more each time. The main point of this exercise is that you let go responsibility for his drinking. Whatever he does is not your fault – or, indeed, anything to do with you. When you can let it go, it sets you free. You can enjoy parties and nights out much more than before when you are not taking responsibility for him, and then try to resist the impulse to rescue him or take on his guilt.

You may find that, now that he has to take responsibility for himself, he tends to be more careful about his drinking. In the past he may also have blamed you for getting drunk. *That* conversation may have been a trigger point for him: "If you hadn't nagged me, I would have been fine." Whether or not that is true is immaterial because now he won't have that excuse.

Renew friendships

You have probably lost touch with friends as the drinking got worse, and with it the guilt and the shame. If you place the guilt and shame back where it actually belongs – with him – then there is no reason why you can't pick up some of the old friendships.

Regardless of how well we believe that we have hidden drink problems from our friends and relations, they generally know. They may not know the detail or the extent of the problem, but they will have a fair idea that there is a problem and that his drinking is at the heart of it. So, re-establishing friendships should be easier than you imagine.

There is another huge advantage to looking up old friends. Friends are a great source of support. If they already know about the alcohol problem, then they may be willing to provide an ear when you need to talk, a shoulder to cry on, and relief from your isolation by providing the comfort of knowing that someone is there should you need them.

Friends can provide so much more because they take us out of ourselves. They can provide an outside interest and relief from some of the obsessive rumination about what he is doing now. There is no doubt that if we have nothing to do to relieve our worry and provide a distraction, our problems magnify. Our friends can provide that distraction. Equally important, they can also provide a sense of perspective.

If you are isolated, it is all too easy to believe that you are the only one with problems, that everyone else has perfect lives. Intellectually and logically, you may know that this is not true, but emotionally you may feel otherwise. Few people, if any, have perfect lives. Most people have some sort of problems – some larger and some smaller than yours. When we mix with people, we are exposed to this truth. It does not remove our problems but it can help us to get them into proportion.

Hobbies or interests

Did you ever have hobbies or sports that you enjoyed? These may have been interests that you engaged in by yourself rather than with the drinker, although he may have participated. Are there things that interest you now but you have been unable to do? You may be interested in a sport (swimming, walking), a course (creative writing, computing), or learning a new skill (pottery, art) – the list is endless.

When you start to let go of responsibility for your drinker, this is a good time to start to build in other things. You are suddenly going to have free time on your hands, something that may not have happened for a few years. Take this time and use it for yourself; treat yourself by doing something that you have always wanted to do.

Why would you want to do this?

Well, first of all, you might just enjoy it! Going out and doing something that you enjoy would seem like an infinitely preferable way of spending your time to waiting around worrying about and looking after a drinker. Getting in touch again with people whose company you appreciate is enjoyable. If enjoyment is not a good enough reason, there are plenty of others.

You could do it for the sake of your health. Staying home, feeling alone and isolated, and worrying about someone else is a recipe for ill health. It is well recognized that people who devote their lives to caring for other people (whether professionally or not) can have emotional and psychological problems. The syndrome is called "burnout", and the main symptoms are extreme fatigue and stress. Another symptom is extreme cynicism, which makes it difficult for sufferers to believe that there is an answer to their dilemma. One way of treating burnout is to take a break (away from the caring situation) and establish some means of social support. If you are feeling very tired and stressed, there is a good chance that you are experiencing burnout. Don't despair, though – this chapter is all about helping you to change.

It is common for people who live with problem drinkers to have very low self-esteem. This is due to many factors. It can be caused by being told you are "useless" on a regular basis when the drinker is drunk. It could be that you view yourself in a negative light. For example, you may feel that if you were a better wife or if he loved you more, then he would not need to drink, and therefore his drinking is your fault. This is a common belief among partners of drinkers and, unfortunately, it suits the drinker to have you believe this. Or you may feel that you should have managed to get him to stop drinking, reduce his drinking, or not get drunk at get-togethers. If your beliefs about yourself fall into any of these categories, then it is unsurprising that your self-esteem is low.

Removing yourself from the situation and handing back responsibility for the drinking and its consequences can help considerably. Being with people who are more affirming is also very helpful.

You may feel boring and uninteresting. Your drinker may help you feel this way by telling you that is part of the reason why he drinks. We don't believe that this is a genuine excuse for him drinking, but if you don't go out anywhere and don't have any hobbies or interests, then perhaps you have limited horizons. Going out and doing something new and interesting brings some variety into your life and conversation, and would make you more stimulating to yourself and your friends. It may also make you more interesting to him.

The fact that you are going out means that you are more likely to make an effort with your appearance as well, and, again, he may see you as more attractive. Also, the fact that you are not there all the time waiting for him, and on him, might rekindle his interest and attention.

Independence

Making more of a life outside the home will help you become more independent. You will build up a social network as you re-establish some friendships. If your drinker does not change in the near future, or indeed at all, these friendships and support will be important to you.

Unfortunately, many relationships with a drinker end in separation or divorce. This may not be something that you wish to contemplate. Many people who live with problem drinkers have a very ambivalent relationship with them. They may hate the way they are living but are terrified of losing the drinker because they love him deeply. That fear may have been a contributory factor to the current situation and may continue to prevent effective intervention. You may be afraid of pushing issues too far in case he leaves. This can result in a lowering of self-esteem and self-respect, and the drinker can also lose respect for you. Thus, paradoxically, the more you fear losing him, the more likely your fears will be realized. Conversely, the more independent you become, the more likely that fear is to diminish and the greater the chances are that he will regain his respect for you.

Others may also benefit from your new hobbies and independence. If you are starting to find a life outside of the home that relieves your stress and makes you happy, then your emotional state will improve. You may find that currently, between the isolation and the continual stress, you have become emotionally volatile. You may find that you are getting angry about things that in the past would not have bothered you at all. You may be overreacting to your partner and your children, and you may feel weepy and tense all the time.

If you are getting away from these stressors on a regular basis and have the support of some friends, then you, and your family, may find that your mood is much more stable. The home may be a happier place to be, and you may find that you are removing yet another of your partner's excuses to drink.

Even if you have young children and babysitting is a problem, there are many opportunities on the internet. You could enrol on a distance learning course or pursue a hobby online. You may be stuck at home, but that does not mean that you can't reach beyond your restrictions.

As you can see, there are many good reasons to look after yourself and to make a more independent life outside of the home. Some of these reasons are about your own well-being and happiness, which are good reasons in themselves. Other reasons are that you make yourself more attractive and interesting to the drinker. Looking after yourself fits well with LOVE. Also, as you embrace more fully a commitment to yourself and your environment, your partner cannot fail to notice the difference and be drawn toward the person with whom he first fell in love.

CHAPTER 13

Surviving the emotional rollercoaster

There is little doubt that living with a problem drinker can be an emotional rollercoaster, and our hearts go out to you because this can be both distressing and exhausting. At times you probably feel that you are lurching from crisis to disaster to crisis again. In this chapter we look at some of the emotions that you may experience living with a problem drinker and what steps you can take to handle these emotions. Many of the emotions may feel the same and the distinction between them unclear. It is our hope that this chapter will help you to unpack these emotions with more clarity and therefore process them more easily.

Disappointment

If you live with a problem drinker, you will almost certainly have experienced a considerable degree of disappointment. Life may have felt like a pendulum swinging between hope and disappointment, highs and lows, breakthroughs and setbacks, until you are tempted either to become the world's greatest cynic or to numb your feelings altogether in despair.

If your partner is a binge drinker, there may be a point in his cycle when he seems to truly want to, and believes he will, stop drinking. He may tell you that this is the end of his drinking and that he is definitely going to change, and if he truly believes it, maybe at this stage so will you. Sadly, though, a subconscious deeper belief may emerge: that he can't cope without his alcohol. So the whole cycle begins all over again. Hope is dashed and disappointment floods your heart (again).

If your partner drinks steadily, it is likely he thinks (or hopes) that no one notices. Then, perhaps, an odd remark from one of his friends shows that people are noticing his high alcohol intake. Maybe he makes a really bad mistake at work that he only just covers up in time. Worried that his world is falling apart, he cuts back his drinking. For a few days (maybe longer) you notice he is no longer drinking as much. Hope begins to build. Maybe this time he will stop altogether. Sadly, this is usually only a temporary lull. His drinking gradually returns and becomes as bad as it was, perhaps even worse. Hope is dashed and disappointment floods the heart (again).

Then there are times when – because he really does love you and the children – he will go with you to see the doctor. He will agree to take the medication, visit the counsellor you arrange for him, attend AA meetings, maybe even for some weeks. When these times come to nothing, he stops attending AA, the counselling doesn't seem to be helping, and you find he's not taking his medication. Then the disappointment feels almost unbearable. "This time," you had said to yourself, "this time I think we'll get there." To see the dream die again feels unbearable! You are furious at him, and furious at yourself for daring to hope that things would be different.

These are just some of the scenarios that will be familiar to you. We're sure you have your own particular tale to tell.

So how can you avoid feeling so disappointed and disillusioned? One thing that will make a real difference is managing your expectations so that they are realistic. If all your hopes are centred around your partner cutting down or stopping his drinking, then it is likely you will be disappointed over and over again. What makes much more sense is to put your energy and attention into the things that are achievable, things that are within your own control. These are goals that are possible, strategies that are sustainable, because they depend on *your* choices and decisions.

If you feel that you have been weighed down by years of disappointment, then first of all we would convey to you compassion and understanding. We would also urge you from now on to put your energies into an area of life fully open to growth and change. You!

As you implement LOVE, HOPE, and SHARE, you will still need patience. You are living with someone whose life is often chaotic, and it would be naive to promise that everything will be plain sailing from now on. Take your eyes off his drinking, but continue to hope for cooperation and communication with your partner. It may sometimes feel like three steps forward and two steps back, but that is still progress. Learn to run with the things that are working and leave the rest for some other time.

Frustration

Closely related to disappointment and anger (which we will discuss in the next section) is frustration. Frustration occurs when there are obstacles preventing us from achieving what we want. That is certainly the case with someone living with a problem drinker because it can feel as if almost everything you are trying to do is thwarted by your drinker.

One of the features of frustration is the tendency to blame ourselves for lack of progress or failure to achieve our goals. This appears to stem from the fact that the types of things that make us frustrated are things that we believe we should be able to do – for example, make the drinker change. Another feature of frustration is that it often leads to repeated, and often more vigorous, attempts to achieve the goal. Imagine you were on an assault course and you had a wall to climb. Everyone else has climbed the wall and you keep getting close to the top but then fall off. A common reaction to this is to take a progressively longer run up and try to jump higher. So as you continue to fail, your attempts become increasingly desperate, until you finally manage to climb the wall. Frustration is not always a negative force, as this example shows.

However, where your situation differs is that, unlike the wall, the drinker is not a passive object. Instead of standing there passively until you can wear him down, he reacts to your continual attempts to get him to change. It would be a bit like the wall increasing its height as you got closer to the top. You feel that you should be able to change him, you get frustrated when you don't get the result that you are looking for, and you redouble your efforts. But that is still not enough.

In your belief that you can change him, you use a number of different strategies – what we have called the 4 Ps (see Chapter 3). But, as we have said before, punishing, picking a fight, policing, and pleading are the equivalent of taking a longer run at the wall. You feel that it should work. If only!

This is where HOPE, LOVE, and SHARE come into their own. LOVE in particular frees you from the assumed responsibility of caretaking for the drinker. As one woman told us recently, she was frustrated trying to manage the drinker, but now the more she withdraws from the drinker, the more he wants to tell her how much he is changing. The way to reduce your frustration is to change what you can and stop trying to change what you can't.

Anger

When you live with a problem drinker, anger is an occupational hazard. A certain amount of anger is natural and even healthy, but too much anger can be destructive. It can eat us up and make it difficult to relate not just to the drinker but also to other people. It can isolate us and remove our main means of support – our friends and relatives. Let's look at what anger is, the different styles of anger, and how to deal with anger. Before we do that, however, it would be useful to clear up one extremely large myth.

"No one makes you angry; you can only allow yourself to be angry." This is one of those trite sayings that has a grain of truth and has been turned into a mainstay of the self-help equivalent of a snake oil salesman. Yes, there are certain ways that you can reduce your susceptibility to frustration and anger, but some people will still manage, deliberately or not, to make us angry. Statements like the one above just increase the guilt and low self-esteem of vulnerable people and can be really unhelpful. Unless you are dead from the neck up, you are going to react occasionally to circumstances. So forget that pronouncement. It rarely works with real people with real problems.

Anger is feeling mad in response to frustration or injury. For example, you don't like what has happened and usually you'd like to get revenge. Anger is an emotional–physiological–cognitive internal state; that means that although we tend to think of it as an emotional state, it is also physical and psychological. Anger causes chemicals (adrenaline and noradrenaline) to course through your body, and your mind and attitude are also involved. It is a complex state. In some instances, angry emotions are healthy; if we are being taken advantage of, anger motivates us to take action (not necessarily aggressive) to correct the situation. This is healthy because it prevents us becoming victims. It is also healthy to be angry in the face of injustice, for ourselves or others.

Anger can sometimes lead to aggression. Where anger is feeling mad, aggression is action – attacking someone or a group. It is intended to harm someone. It can be a verbal attack – insults, threats, sarcasm, or attributing nasty motives to other people – or a physical punishment or restriction. Aggression is different from assertiveness, which is tactfully and rationally standing up for our rights. Indeed, assertiveness is designed *not* to hurt others. SHARE and LOVE are based on assertiveness.

Controlling anger

Maintaining your calm and controlling your anger when you live with a problem drinker may not be an impossible task but it is certainly a very difficult one. Here are seven strategies to help:

1. Take responsibility for your feelings in order to avoid blaming others. Anger is less likely to escalate into full-blown arguments if you use start with "I feel" rather than "You". For example, "I feel angry when you are twenty minutes late and you don't call me" is much better than "You make me so mad by being late."

2. Wait a few days to cool down emotionally when a situation makes you feel wild with intense feelings such as rage. As time passes, you will be able to be more objective about the issues and sort out your feelings about the situation more clearly.

3. Make a decision to speak respectfully whenever you are angry or frustrated. You are much more likely to have your issues heard. (Lou found this was the wisest – but also the hardest – strategy when she was living with her first husband. Whenever she managed to do it, however, the situation became much easier.)

4. It is an old solution but it works: count to ten. That gives you time to think and bite back the words that may have been on the tip of your tongue.

5. Another old solution is to take yourself for a walk when you are beginning to feel tense and the anger is rising. Absenting yourself from the cause of your

anger and having time to think are useful strategies.

6. If you can manage it, injecting humour into the situation is a good way to defuse any tense situation. It is very difficult to maintain your anger when you laugh. Of course, it is not always easy to see the funny side of things.

7. Lastly, share with supportive individuals who may give you, if not good advice, then at least a sympathetic ear. Being heard can defuse the initial intensity of your anger and help the feeling become more manageable.

Anxiety and worry

Living with a drinker, you will almost certainly know all about anxiety. At first you might have worried about when he would come home and what state he would be in. After a while you might have found yourself worrying about just about everything. You probably find it difficult to relax, that you are tense and jumpy, that your heart races and your hands sweat. You might also find it difficult to concentrate and remember things. These are all common symptoms of anxiety. Prolonged periods of worry and anxiety can undermine your health and leave you with chronic illness or fatigue.

There are many theories of anxiety – what causes it and how to treat it. However, the cause is not too difficult to find for someone living with a problem drinker. Constant and consistent exposure to the stressful and chaotic behaviour of the drinker means that it is difficult to switch off to what is happening, and it probably feels as if the anxiety and worry just snowball till they take over your life completely.

So what can you do about it?

As with anything that causes anxiety, the ideal solution is to remove yourself from the situation so that his behaviour does not affect you any more. There are probably many reasons why that may be unrealistic and impractical, and you may also be very committed to staying in the relationship. Even if you cannot remove yourself physically, however, you could remove yourself emotionally from the situation. As we have said many times in this book, detaching from the situation is helpful for both the drinker and yourself. Using LOVE and SHARE, you can both detach and gain some mastery over your circumstances. Here are some other general strategies that help with anxiety and worry.

- Exercise is a great tension reliever. Not only does it help you to burn off some of the chemicals that are associated with anxiety and anger, but it also releases other chemicals (endorphins) that make you feel good. It increases fitness levels and helps with tiredness.

- Sharing with others is useful. Having a support network so that you can unburden yourself without feeling self-conscious is a good way of discharging your anxiety. You may also look at techniques such as relaxation CDs and visualization. Having a quiet place that you can escape to can help relieve anxiety. Nature has great healing qualities. A walk in the country, at the seaside, or in a local park can soothe jangled nerves and calm a troubled mind.

- If you feel that it is impossible to stop worrying altogether, then you could try a different technique. Decide that you are going to continue to worry but limit it. So, for example, allow yourself half an hour a day to worry. Find a place to sit and worry about everything that is bothering you. Then decide that you will not worry again outside that time. If you do start to worry about something, note it down for your next worry session. If you worry all the time, then you probably think that this is pretty ridiculous. It is a way to start to control your worry, but, like most techniques, it takes time and effort.

• Finally, do remember that seeing a therapist or counsellor to talk through your concerns can ease the burden of worry quite considerably.

Depression

Depression is one of the most common mental health disorders and perhaps one of the most misunderstood. Many people talk about being "depressed" when what they really mean is that they are feeling sad, fed up, or just generally low in mood. These passing feelings are something that most of us experience from time to time. Sometimes there is a very good reason and sometimes there is no obvious reason at all. The point is that it is a transient feeling that may last an hour, a day, or a couple of days. Depression, on the other hand, is a condition that can last for months and even years.

Depression can be caused by physical illness, or a person can be genetically predisposed to the condition. For others it can be caused by stress and is commonly found with anxiety. Living with a problem drinker is a fertile environment for depression. You live with fairly unremitting stress that saps your energy, you feel guilty, you feel powerless, and your self-esteem is probably low and takes a regular beating. In such a situation it would not be very surprising to find that depression flourishes.

Symptoms of depression are:

- constant feelings of sadness, irritability, or tension that last for more than a month

- no interest or pleasure in usual activities or hobbies

- loss of energy or feeling tired, despite not doing much

- a change in appetite: losing or gaining weight

- a change in sleeping patterns, such as difficulty sleeping, early morning awakening, or sleeping too much

- restlessness or feeling slowed down

- difficulty making decisions or concentrating

- feelings of worthlessness, hopelessness, or guilt

- thoughts of suicide or death.

So, what can you do about it? First of all, if you believe that you have depression and are showing some or all of the symptoms listed above, go and see your doctor. Depression can be treated and there is a very good prognosis, especially if treated early. There are things that you can do for yourself. The first thing a doctor would suggest is to avoid stress. Easier said than done with a problem drinker around. However, you could use LOVE and SHARE to reduce the stress as much as you can. Try doing things that you enjoy. You could combine that with looking up old friends and helping yourself through a supportive network. Take some exercise. There is some research evidence that the endorphins you generate during exercise can be beneficial to depression. In fact, they are said to be beneficial to all of us, depressed or not. If you can, avoid making major decisions in your life until the depression lifts.

Living with a problem drinker can take its toll, physically and emotionally. Caretaking for your drinker can cause you enormous stress and psychological problems. Most of these problems can be eased at least a little by using the tools of this book, HOPE, LOVE, and SHARE. However, they are not a panacea for all problems. If you find yourself with enduring depression or find your life blighted by anxiety, then visit your doctor and/or see a counsellor. There is help available; don't be afraid to ask for it or use it.

Obviously, we have only been able to scratch the surface in our look at these areas. There are many useful books available that will unpack these issues in greater detail.

CHAPTER 14

Where to find help

A common observation is that almost all of the help that is available seems to be focused on the problem drinker; there is very little help for the family. It was that sense of inequality that brought us to start the *Bottled Up* project. We have both had the experience of talking to wives, husbands, sons and daughters, mothers and fathers of drinkers and hearing their sense of abandonment and desperation. Although this is a reasonably valid observation, there are resources out there; there are people and organizations that can and will help if you seek them out. This chapter will discuss what is available.

Family doctor

The first port of call for anyone experiencing problems with another's drinking should be the family doctor. For some of you, the doctor will be like part of your extended family, having known you for many years, maybe even from your childhood. For others, the acquaintance may be much more recent. In both cases it can be difficult to approach your doctor, as you may be embarrassed or ashamed to bring up the subject. Nevertheless, it is worth talking to a professional about your situation. The doctor will have information about local help or support groups. There may be sources of support you never considered that you could access.

In recent years in the UK, and in other countries, there has been a move toward family doctors being the front line for tackling alcohol problems. This has happened as healthcare systems have increasingly recognized the costs incurred through people's drinking. Some doctors are not always comfortable with this new role and are not always diligent about approaching the topic; nevertheless, given good reason, most doctors will raise the issue with a client. So, if you discuss the situation with your doctor, then, the next time your drinker visits the surgery, your doctor can raise the issue with him formally and perhaps suggest treatment or other options for reducing drinking.

Your doctor can help you in other ways. As we have discussed, living with a drinker can lead to psychological problems such as depression, stress, and anxiety. If required, your doctor can prescribe medication (for example, antidepressants or anxiolytics) that can help you. Alternatively, you may require other types of medication to build you up (a tonic, for example) or to help to strengthen your constitution. In addition, many medical practices have established partnerships with counsellors and therapists. Your doctor can refer you to someone who can listen to your situation and help you to find a pathway through some of the problems you are facing.

Treatment centres

It could be worth contacting a local treatment centre if there is one. Some, but by no means all, will have support groups or even supportive staff to help the families of problem drinkers. This is one of those resources that is mainly aimed at the drinkers, with little offered for families. Some treatment facilities do offer family therapy; however, you should be aware that generally they will treat the drinker within a "systems theory" approach. What that means is that you are viewed as part of the behavioural system within which the drinker drinks or feels the need to drink; your own personal issues are unlikely to be addressed.

Whether or not a treatment facility supports the families of drinkers tends to depend on the management, but generally they do not provide that support as a matter of course. However, it is worthwhile exploring what help they do provide; after all, you hope that your drinker will be making contact with them soon.

Al-Anon

Probably one of the better-known sources of help and support is Al-Anon, the family groups of Alcoholics Anonymous (A A). Like A A, Al-Anon is a fellowship of men and women who offer mutual support and are guided by the twelve-step programme. Members of Al-Anon are people who live with a problem drinker. Similar to A A, there is no professional input to the meetings (unless the professional is there as an Al-Anon member).

Most large towns in the English-speaking world will have an Al-Anon group, and everyone is welcome. They are also online and many regions will have an online meeting. There is no charge for the meetings, although members are expected to contribute to the running of the Al-Anon group and the wider organization. If they are going to learn about the programme of recovery, members will also have to buy various bits of Al-Anon literature.

Many people attending Al-Anon feel released from guilt and shame. The first step of Al-Anon, and a central tenet of its philosophy, is the concept of being powerless. This states that since you are powerless over alcohol and the alcoholic, you did not cause the problem, you can't control it, and you can't cure it. For some, this is a great relief; for others, less so.

It is clear that both AA and Al-Anon have been a great source of help for many people. Most of their literature is great, and we would recommend anyone to buy some of it and find out for themselves what this organization has to offer. We especially recommend their daily readings books which give guidance over the period of a year and help to build a disciplined approach based on taking it a day at a time.

These are some of the many positives of Al-Anon. For some people, however, there are negatives too. Some find the quasi-religious nature of Al-Anon to be off-putting. There is a continuous round of accusation and refutation that AA and Al-Anon are overly religious in their reliance on a higher power and in their workings. AA and Al-Anon refute the accusation by pointing to their literature which states that AA and Al-Anon offer a *spiritual* rather than a religious programme. The ruling by the Ninth US Circuit Court of Appeals in San Francisco, that it was unconstitutional to send parolees to AA because of its religious nature, has damaged that claim considerably. Regardless of whether it is spiritual or religious, many people have benefitted from the programme and have been comforted by having this higher power.

One of the issues that we at *Bottled Up* have with Al-Anon is its insistence that members accept that they are powerless to affect the drinker. As you have read in this book so far, we insist that you *can* exert an influence on the drinker. We believe that you can control some of the consequences of the drinking through SHARE, and that, through LOVE, you can influence the drinker to engage in more family-oriented activities that do not involve alcohol. We also believe that, by applying this programme, there is a strong possibility that he will change his drinking entirely.

Spiritual help

The addiction treatment and recovery field has been linked to spiritual help for hundreds of years. A couple of centuries ago, inebriety (an old name for alcoholism) was thought by the physicians of the time to be caused by weak morals. They had an old saying, "Spiritus contra spiritum", which is a Latin pun. Translated, it says "Spirit drives out spirit"; in Latin the words for "alcohol" and "spirituality" are the same. So what this means is that spirits (alcohol) make someone morally weak, and that spirit (God) drives out alcohol. Thus, it was widely believed that alcohol and spirituality were interlinked in both cause and cure. Indeed, in the eighteenth century it was considered that the only cure for inebriety was to become more moral and accept God. Courts would give drunks the alternative of living with a minister for a year or going to prison and/or receiving a whipping.

Years later, in 1935, Bill Wilson (a founder of AA) was taken to a meeting of a religious organization called the Oxford Group, and that was where he established the foundation of his sobriety. He later left the Oxford Group and went on to establish AA. However, he borrowed their programme of seven steps, later to be expanded into the twelve steps of AA. Since then, many spiritual and religious organizations have helped people to recover using either a modified version of the twelve steps or straightforward spiritual principles.

For many people today, there is a tendency to move away from anything overtly advocating or even hinting at religion or spirituality. This is not a universal tendency, however. In some areas of medical research – for example, how people cope with cancer and aging – it is recognized that there is something at work that is beyond the understanding of science. Eighteenth-century physicians would probably recognize this "holistic" approach to medicine.

So, how does this help you?

Many, many people believe there is a God and that he cares about humankind. Some people put it another way: that there is a spiritual force, a force for good, that we can tap into and experience. This is good news. In this secretive, unstable, demanding world in which we live, there is, somewhere, somebody we can come to. Someone greater than ourselves can enter our world and begin to help us. Of course, if there is a God, Divine Power, Higher Being, or whatever title is familiar to you, then the next question you may ask is this: "How can I make contact with this God?"

All of the help that we have suggested up to this point can easily be found in the *Yellow Pages* and is only a phone call away. In the UK at least, God does not have a listing in the *Yellow Pages*. However, contact is not that difficult if you want to make it. There are two possibilities. The first is very simple: just speak to God in a place and in a way that you find comfortable. Some people have done this and their lives have been profoundly changed. There is little to lose and could be much to gain. If you decide to talk to God or pray, you could try the prayer written by the American theologian Reinhold Niebuhr, adopted by the twelve-step fraternity and said at most A A and Al-Anon meetings. Most people know it as the Serenity Prayer:

God,
grant me the serenity
to accept the things I cannot change;
courage to change the things I can;
and the wisdom to know the difference.

The second method is a bit more formal but could come with extra benefits. Many people have found support and encouragement in church. Often priests and ministers have training in helping people with life problems.

Both Lou and John found that a spiritual faith helped them to deal with their respective alcohol problems. Lou found great comfort in prayer when her husband was drinking and when she was trying to cope with his unpredictability. John found a faith as part of his recovery in A A.

In conclusion, although there is not a huge amount of support for families, what is there is nevertheless significant. Your family doctor can help with your health problems and may be able to influence your drinker. Your local treatment facility may run support groups or have dedicated counsellors. There is, of course, Al-Anon, the family groups of A A. Many find comfort in prayer and spiritual beliefs, and they can find support through a church community. Finally, you may want to look on the internet for support groups. Al-Anon, for example, has meetings and resources online, as have other family support groups such as Alateen and some non-twelve-step groups. So too does *Bottled Up*.

CHAPTER 15

Recovery?

We write this chapter knowing that even to attempt to cover the subject of recovery fully would take an entire book. For now, here is a discussion of some of the main themes surrounding the issue.

You have HOPED, LOVED, and SHARED, and, we hope, your drinker has changed his drinking behaviour; in fact, he may even have stopped completely. So everything is now great. Or is it? We sincerely hope that it is great or at least that there has been an improvement on how you were living previously. For most of you, unfortunately, it is likely that there is still a considerable amount of work to be done if the relationship is going to thrive. Remember that there has been a lot of mistrust and emotional and perhaps even physical damage over the years. There have been arguments, promises made, promises broken, hopes raised, and hopes dashed. These things take time to heal. There are also the problems that can arise from the adjustment to a new way of life for both you and the drinker.

The issues we discuss below may not affect all of you or will not affect you all to the same extent. If the drinking problem is recent and has been short-lived, then these problems and subsequent adjustments may be fairly mild. However, if the drinking problem has been an established pattern for many years, then having a non-drinker as a partner will be a whole new experience, to which you, your partner, and your family will need to adjust. And, as you have already experienced, change is seldom easy.

This chapter and the issues discussed in it are not meant in any way to dissuade you from trying to change your drinker and yourself. Quite the reverse! We want your new relationship status to continue as problem-free as possible. We are discussing these issues to forewarn you of the possible pitfalls, so that you will not find them spoiling your happiness. It is unlikely that all the issues you meet in rebuilding your relationship will come from just one of you. It is much more likely that you will both have adjustment issues that will arise from your experience and hopes for the future. So the first issue we will discuss is expectations.

Unrealistic expectations

It has been difficult hanging on and keeping the faith over the years. You may have spent quite a lot of time dreaming about when he stops drinking and your life gets back to normal. You may have very definite ideas what that "normal" will entail.

One of the dangers here is that you may set yourself up for disappointment. It may be that your expectations, although understandable, are unrealistic. It is possible that you have a vision of family life that is not shared by your partner or that he cannot deliver even if he does share it. It may also be the case that he doesn't actually know what your dream is. Over the years your communication has almost certainly suffered; that is something that needs to be repaired. Talking through what you both want and expect from each other may be revealing and help to clarify your new roles and status. It may be difficult at first because you are probably not accustomed to sitting and planning together. We hope that your recent experience of working through the *Bottled Up* programme and using HOPE, LOVE, and SHARE to discuss your hopes and wishes will help you with this step.

Rather than having high expectations, you may find yourself at the other extreme. Having been disappointed so many times, you may feel reluctant to allow your hopes to be built up too far as it is painful to have them crushed again. Indeed, you may take the view that having no hope is easier to deal with because it is a state that, though not comfortable, is at least familiar.

Again, this is an understandable reaction to the rollercoaster ride of uncertainty that has been your life. However, beware that you don't become too cynical. He probably needs support, especially in the early days of recovery, and so he may take your negativity as a sign that you don't believe in him or appreciate the changes he has made, or that you just don't care. It is important to stress that it is not your responsibility to keep him sober, but it is in your interests to provide him with support and encouragement.

Walking on eggshells

You may find that your ex-drinker is experiencing difficulty adjusting to his new sober lifestyle and you feel that he is reacting irritably to any interaction. This does not mean that you need to monitor your every word or action in case he becomes negative and has a drink. Some people describe this as walking on eggshells. It is a very uncomfortable way to live. In fact, if you are living like this, then you probably feel that it is not very different from when he was drinking. For you, nothing very much has changed. We are sure that this is not what you dreamed of or hoped for when he got sober.

If you feel that you are walking on eggshells, perhaps start by asking yourself why you are doing that. Remember LOVE. In introducing LOVE, we urged you to try to stop caretaking or policing his drinking and to put the responsibility back where it belongs – with him. Look at your own behaviour and try to ensure that you are not returning to old patterns of behaviour now that he has stopped. You know from experience that worrying about his drinking and policing him never got him sober. So it is unlikely that worrying about whether he is going to drink will *keep* him sober!

Obviously, you do not want him to return to drinking and all the misery that brought. Remember, though, that you are not responsible for him staying sober or drinking. If he drinks, it is completely his choice! By all means, as we said above, be supportive and positive, but remember that you have a life as well and you should live it. Besides, he needs to take responsibility and that can be difficult if you are fussing around him. Letting him get on with his recovery may be the best thing for both of you and will allow you both to grow.

Getting to know each other again

As you no doubt already know, drinking heavily for long periods of time changes people. So too does living with the drinker during this period. Even if for no other reason, time passes and people get older. However, it is more than that. Roles can also change through time, as we will discuss in the next section. Now that he has stopped drinking, you will almost certainly need to spend time finding out about each other again. In fact, you may need to spend some time getting to know *yourselves*.

One of the first times Lou and I (John) met again after many years was illuminating. We were driving in the car and I asked her what she wanted from her future. She looked at me as if I was speaking a foreign language and eventually said that she did not know. This was not the answer I expected, as the Lou I had known many years before appeared to know exactly what she wanted from life. She later told me she had not thought about what she wanted for herself for so long that she had not known how to answer the question. Unfortunately, that can happen when living with a drinker. Your horizons can become narrowed to the extent that it feels that you are constantly firefighting; that you are either dealing with the latest crisis or gearing up for the next one. For those reasons, you don't actually have thoughts about what you want for yourself or for the future. If there are children involved, then the situation becomes even more complicated as their needs and safety will also take precedence over yours. So knowing now what you want may be more difficult than you first appreciate.

This can affect your drinker as well. Drinkers, particularly dependent drinkers, can find that they are strangers to themselves when they sober up. In their drinking days, emotions, good or bad, were regularly reduced to a state of intoxication: "I feel good, so I'll drink; I feel bad, so I'll drink." The result was that no emotion or physical state was felt long enough to make an impact. Other interests, hobbies, and sports were all dropped because they interfered with drinking time. So when drinkers sober up, they often don't know what they like or dislike, how to handle emotions, or what kind of interests they have.

So, again, you may need to spend some time getting to know yourselves and each other. This could be an adventure. It might seem like a strange kind of adventure, especially if you have been with this person for twenty or thirty years. You have both almost certainly changed quite considerably in that time, so do not expect to find the same person you first met. You may find that he is now someone you like even better!

Rebuilding your relationship and family life

Just as you may need to spend time getting to know each other, you will probably have to spend time rebuilding a family life. Having someone who is around more often can be a mixed blessing. Someone quipped to us recently about their new stage of retirement, "I married him for better or worse, but not for lunch."

Until now you have probably had the responsibility of the home, the shopping, the cooking, and raising the children. You may have longed for the help of your partner to take some of the responsibility off your shoulders, to help with the children when they were being difficult or going through problem times in their adolescence. Having a sober partner back might seem like a great result and be what you have dreamed of. However, often the reality is less attractive than the dream. For some years the responsibility of the home and children may have been a burden for you, although one you probably readily accepted. That has most likely meant you have also had a free hand to make the decisions.

Now that he is sober, he may want to influence decisions or, even worse, make them himself. "That is what I dreamed about," you might say. "I have longed for him to take responsibility and free me up. I have wanted him to take over some of the duties of rearing the family, organizing the finances, and other duties I have been carrying for years."

Sounds like a result! But let us ask a question. What if he decides to change things? What if his ideas about child-rearing are different from yours? What if he is much more liberal or much stricter? What if he decides that your money will be spent differently, or disagrees with how much you are spending on the groceries and wants to budget in a quite different way? How are you going to feel about these kinds of changes? Are you going to be able to stand back, breathe a sigh of relief, and say "Thank you, dear, for coming to rescue me"? Or are you going to feel aggrieved that you have been doing this without his help for years and insulted that he is now criticizing your efforts? Will you accept it gratefully, or will you tell him in no uncertain terms where to get off?

This may sound like the plot for a sitcom, but unfortunately this situation is all too common in a recovery home. The roles become blurred and confused as the drinker avoids his responsibilities and the partner has to cope with looking after the children and keeping the home afloat. When the drinker gets sober, sometimes he can upset this situation. This can be done for benign reasons but in a tactless way. He may genuinely be trying to take up the responsibilities that he acknowledges he has avoided. He may actually be trying to help. However, if he does not discuss it with his partner at some length and ask what she might like him to do, then her reception of him could be rather different to the one he expects.

Rather than seeing him as a knight in shining armour riding to your rescue, you could become extremely defensive. You may feel that your territory has been invaded. For this to be resolved amicably, you both need to stand back and see the other's point of view, instead of becoming locked in a power struggle. It is not easy, but the more you can do it, the more you will get from the relationship. This is a conflict that is well worth weathering as the outcome could be a more balanced partnership and an opportunity for more space and time.

In a similar vein, your partner's return may not be welcomed by the children. Often when Dad is a drinker, he can be manipulated in his sobering-up moments between binges when he is wracked with guilt and remorse. If the children learned how to play him, then they could have got him to part with money, gifts, or concessions that they would not have got otherwise. Now that he is sober, they might lose the gravy train. They might also be very resentful of his drinking behaviour and the things that he has or hasn't done. They might resist his attempts to bond or exercise authority now that he is sober. Beware of getting caught in the crossfire and having to take sides or appear to take sides. If you can, try to be the peacemaker. If you can't, don't despair; time may heal the rift.

He may spend time on other pursuits

One not unreasonable expectation that you probably have is that you will spend more time together. Previously, he had probably spent a lot of time elsewhere – for example, in the bar. Even if he was around, he probably did not join in or enhance family life. Now you want some family life with him being around and sober.

If he got sober by going to AA, then that might be another expectation that is not realized. A common complaint when people get sober through AA is that they go from people who would not be seen dead at an AA meeting to being at meetings on a nightly basis. I (John) remember the very first AA meeting I went to (incidentally it was also the last for some time as I hated it then). I asked the AA member who picked me up how often he went to these meetings and he said that he attended every night. So I asked him what his wife thought. He said that she was really glad he was sober. So I asked him how she knew he was sober, because it seemed to me that she might have seen more of him when he was drinking.

Around five years later, the same criticism was made of me by my own wife: I was spending too much time at meetings and with AA members. There is a feeling of identity and belonging in AA that can be very appealing for a recovering problem drinker. It does mean, however, that he is spending less time at home at the very time of the evening when the family is around. I should stress that although this is fairly common, it does not happen with everyone, and when it does happen, it tends to happen to the newer members. This is probably because this is the time when they most need and appreciate the group's support.

Sometimes recovering drinkers can spend too much time on other pursuits, albeit healthy ones. For example, he may find that when he stops drinking he is very unfit and has a beer belly. As part of his recovery he might join a gym or a sports club (for example, golf) and then spend huge amounts of time getting fit or playing golf.[1] This is all very commendable as he will be dealing with his fitness and any weight problem. He will be spending his time doing things that keep him away from alcohol and keep him healthy. However, as far as you and the family are concerned, you may be spending as little time with him as you were when he was drinking.

You already have the tools to change this behaviour, and you have the experience of using them. Just as before when you tried to change his drinking, you can use SHARE and LOVE to assess and then tell him about the consequences of his behaviour – and provide alternatives. Again, you may need to give him reasons to spend time with you and the family.

That last statement may have made you angry. Why should you be the one making the effort *again*? You are his partner and family; that is more than enough reason to spend time with you. No argument from us. As we

---

1 Some people have pointed to this almost obsessive type of behaviour (for example, going to A A meetings or participating in sport) as proof of an addictive personality.

have continually said in this section, however, this is a new situation, and if it is going be successful, perhaps you need to take the initiative for a bit longer. Part of the discussion you have will be stating your hopes for your new relationship and your expectations of each other. Think of this work as a bank account; you are making deposits now so that you can make withdrawals or live on the interest later.

Re-evaluate your life and relationship

As you work your way through the *Bottled Up* programme, you will start to see things in a different light. As you assess the consequences of drinking on your life in a different way, you will inevitably start to look at your life, relationship, and yourself from a new perspective. Now that you have moved to a new phase in your life where your partner is sober and your life is changing, you could find yourself re-evaluating your life and the people in it. You may feel that you want more change than has happened already. You may find that you want your ex-drinker and the rest of your family to start doing things for which, up till now, you have taken responsibility. It is even possible that you will start to feel discontent with your life.

Some of this may be a reaction to change. All choices entail selection and rejection, and you might find yourself fantasizing about what your life might have been like if, instead of being with your ex-drinker, you had married that guy who always fancied you. The point is that you will never know.

Be prepared that, after the crisis has died down and the drinking has stopped, you might find that you have waves of sadness and regret. If this happens, you may be mourning the life that never was, the death of a dream of what your life might have been. You looked at some of this in SHARE when you assessed the impact of drinking on your ambitions and hopes. If you start to experience a deep sadness, don't let people dismiss these feelings as being maudlin or self-pitying. They are very real; you are experiencing grief for your lost aspirations.

You can never recapture those dreams, but you can make new ones. They may not start from where you were years ago when life was so full of promise, but that does not mean that your dreams cannot be exciting and fulfilling. For that to happen, however, maybe you need to learn to dream again. Maybe you need to learn to trust that your life is not going to suddenly implode, plunging you into a crisis as he gets drunk again. Rebuilding that trust takes time.

Just as you are re-evaluating your life, so too your ex-drinker may be examining his. Just as you may have found your life wanting, so your ex-drinker may feel the same about his life, and maybe also you. This is a process that partners and families feel is very unfair, and in most cases justifiably so. You have been there through all his drinking, cleaned up after him, protected him, isolated yourself for his sake. Yes, we know. However, he is probably going through a similar process to the one you may be going through. All behaviour change requires a re-examination of ourselves and our lives, so he will be looking at his life and trying to figure out where he is going. This does not make it any easier for you, especially if he voices his doubts.

For all the above reasons, some relationships that

survived the drinking don't survive the recovery. Some of the changes in roles and changes of personality (for example, he may have mood swings or be miserable and bad-tempered) are the last straw for the partner. You hung on in the relationship, expecting that it would all be different – and it was, but not in the way you hoped. At the outset of sobriety, the work is not over; it is just beginning. You have achieved the first step of a new life: his drinking behaviour has changed. Now it is time to build a beginning, a life full of possibilities. This will need application, commitment, and time to achieve the results that you hope for. It also takes another quality that we will discuss next – forgiveness.

Forgiveness

If you are going to rebuild a relationship with your ex-drinker, then you need to let go of the anger that you have for his drinking behaviour. The action that sets us free from our anger, hatred, and resentment is forgiveness. For many of us, however, forgiveness can often be hard because we confuse it with other reactions.

Forgiveness is not forgetting about being hurt, nor is it believing that the other person was not guilty or not responsible for the wrong things he did. Forgiveness is not approval of what was done or considering it any less serious or hurtful, and it certainly is not permission to repeat the hurt.

Forgiveness is a decision that you will no longer hate the person or hold a grudge. It is an attempt to heal yourself, to give yourself some peace. Research has found that forgiveness can help people be more at peace with themselves.

To forgive another, it is useful, but not essential, to be able to empathize – that is, to see it from the other's point of view. This might be difficult: you may not be able to understand why he drank so much and so often and could not change. What is really important is your decision that you will no longer be a victim; that you do not want to be defined by the hurt that has been done to you. You decide that you will rise above the hurt and let it go. Forgiveness is about giving up your desire for revenge and the desire to see the other person hurt. Instead, you wish him well. This does not mean, however, that you take on the job of trying to fix him or be his therapist.

By forgiving the drinker, you will start to lose your anger and resentment. As a result, the healing process of the ex-drinker, your family, your relationship, and even yourself will be speeded up and should go more quickly and surely. You will start to feel better about yourself and within yourself as you lose that nagging voice that tells you how much you have been hurt and wants you to dream about getting "justice".

The other person you may need to forgive in this situation is yourself. As we have discussed in earlier chapters, you may blame yourself for the situation. If only you had been stronger, wiser, more attractive, had spoken up sooner... It was his choice to drink. If there is fault in this situation, then the fault is not yours. If you still feel a residual guilt, then it is time to let it go. Forgive yourself. You have an opportunity to look forward and build, rather than looking back and bearing grudges.

Forgiveness is not easy. When Lou is working with her clients, she prefers to use the words "path" or "journey" when referring to forgiveness because it is often something that takes time and is achieved step-by-step, rather than all at once. Sometimes it seems as if the feelings of anger and injustice push the prospect of forgiveness into the background. However, we would urge you to continue until this emotional task is completed. It brings a deeper peace about the past and a greater empowering for love and care in the future.

CHAPTER 16

Change for good

Unless you change how you are, you will always have what you've got.
Jim Rohn

In this book we have introduced you to the *Bottled Up* approach and its tools – HOPE, LOVE, and SHARE. These tools are not a panacea; we make no such claim. Indeed, the very use of the word "tools" usually means that there is work involved, and this approach is certainly no different. There *is* work involved and the work can be hard. The rewards can also be great.

The challenge facing you starts with changing your attitudes to alcohol problems. It is very likely that previously you wanted a definition of alcoholism that was written for your drinker. You felt that this definition was the leverage you needed to get him to change; that, faced with this irrefutable proof, he would see the error of his ways and change his behaviour for ever. We have shown you that you do not need that kind of proof. Most drinking problems (within marriages and close relationships) are also relationship problems. So if you *believe* that it is a problem, it *is* a problem. Have the courage of your convictions.

We have tried to show that part of the problem, and definitely part of the solution, lies in the interaction between yourself and your drinker. You had probably worked your way through the 4 Ps on a number of occasions and become increasingly frustrated and despairing. The *Bottled Up* approach suggests that you move away from this business-as-usual approach and try something different. If you have given the *Bottled Up* approach your best shot, you have almost certainly found differences in your life. They may not be the differences that you set out to find – they may even be unexpected – but we believe that they will be changes for the better.

The first changes we would expect to see are changes within yourself. You are probably aware that your anger and anxiety are receding and that the feelings of powerlessness and helplessness have gone and been replaced with a growing confidence. We believe that you will feel stronger, more able to influence your life. Those changes will, in themselves, have an effect on your drinker as he sees you become more confident and assertive.

We hope that part of the change is within your drinker and his drinking. That may take more time. As we have suggested, it has almost certainly taken a while to establish the pattern of drinking that led to you buying this book and it may take some time to alter that pattern to what you want. However, every change in you is a step toward that outcome, so keep working away at HOPE, LOVE, and SHARE, and things should improve and eventually change will come.

One thing that we sincerely hope has changed is that you are less isolated; that you have taken the advice of this book and created a life for yourself independent of the drinker and outside of the home. We hope that you have a support network of friends and relatives who are there for you; that you have people who will listen when you need to talk and will help to bolster your self-esteem when it crashes. We all need that, whether we live with a drinker or not.

Through applying the information in *Bottled Up*, we hope your life, home, and children will be a bit safer than they were. Things may not yet be comfortable in the way you would like, but we trust that some of the risk has been removed, or at least reduced.

Finally, we anticipate that your relationship with your drinker will improve. Again, it may not yet be the relationship that you had dreamed of, but we hope that it is getting better, that some of the love is returning, and that you are exercising forgiveness, for him and you. As we discussed in Chapter 15, forgiveness is important if you are going to forge a good relationship that lasts.

One thing is certain: if you make a new life with your drinker, or forge your way alone, life can be full of meaning, joy, and new horizons. This is a voyage of discovery, as you re-evaluate who you really are, what you want to do, and the people with whom you want to share your life. A full life is eminently possible and you deserve to find it.

We wish you good luck in this new adventure.

Useful resources

Books for people who live with a problem drinker

Al-Anon Family Groups, *Alateen: A Day at a Time*, Virginia Beach, VA: Al-Anon, 1983.

Al-Anon Family Groups, *One Day at a Time in Al-Anon*, Virginia Beach, VA: An-Anon, 1987.

Melody Beattie, *Codependent No More: How to Stop Controlling Others and Start Caring for Yourself*, Center City, MN: Hazelden Publishing, 1989.

Melody Beattie, *The Language of Letting Go: Daily Meditations for Codependents*, Center City, MN: Hazelden Publishing, 1990.

Robert J. Meyers and Brenda L. Wolfe, *Get Your Loved One Sober: Alternatives to Nagging, Pleading, and Threatening*, Center City, MN: Hazelden Publishing, 2003.

Janet G. Woititz, *Adult Children of Alcoholics*, Deerfield Beach, FL: Health Communications, Inc., 1990.

Books for problem drinkers

Allen Carr, *Allen Carr's Easy Way to Control Alcohol*, Second edition, London: Arcturus Publishing, 2009. John McMahon, *First Steps Out of Problem Drinking*, Oxford: Lion Hudson, 2010.

Websites for people who live with a problem drinker

http://bottled-up.memberlodge.com
www.al-anonuk.org.uk

www.al-anon.alateen.org/alateen
http://acoa.co.uk – Adult Children of Alcoholics

Websites for people with alcohol problems
www.247helpyourself.com
www.alcoholhelponline.com
www.alcoholics-anonymous.org.uk

Information websites about alcohol
www.niaaa.nih.gov – National Institute on Alcohol Abuse and Alcoholism
www.alcohol-and-drug-guide.com
www.nih.gov – National Institutes of Health (US Department of Health and Human Services)